CONTENTS

Ships in Focus Publications

Correspondence and editorial:
Roy Fenton
18 Durrington Avenue
London SW20 8NT
020 8879 3527
rfenton@rfenton.demon.co.uk

Orders and photographic:
John & Marion Clarkson
18 Franklands, Longton
Preston PR4 5PD
01772 612855
shipsinfocus@btinternet.com

Printed by Amadeus Press Ltd., Cleckheaton,
Yorkshire.
Designed by Hugh Smallwood, John Clarkson
and Roy Fenton.

SHIPS IN FOCUS RECORD
ISBN 978-1-901703-90-0

SUBSCRIPTION RATES FOR RECORD

Readers can start their subscription with
any issue, and are welcome to backdate it to
receive previous issues.

	3 issues	4 issues
UK	£24	£31
Europe (airmail)	£26	£34
Rest of the world (surface mail)	£26	£34
Rest of the world (airmail)	£31	£41

SHIPS IN FOCUS
November 2

Most collectors of photographs will have begun by
Quite likely, as interest develops, other views of a s
photographers, in different lighting, from another angle or – most interestingly –
showing modifications or variations in livery. The 'Fleet in Focus' feature on the later
Bibby liners in this issue convinces us of the value of this approach. Bibby vessels
showed a remarkable degree of variation, partly as they were modified for their various
roles, but also because they were frequently chartered out and had their funnels
repainted accordingly. Indeed, in some cases it is only through studying photographs
that a story of modification emerges, especially of liveries, as these are rarely
chronicled in fleet histories. Dated photographs are especially valuable in this respect.

Our policy of aiming to credit both the photographer and the collector of
images we use has been welcomed. To recap on what we wrote previously, we seek
to not only recognise the work of the person behind the camera, but also to thank the
collector who acquired, catalogued, cared for, retrieved and lent us the image (and
will have to put it back when we return it). Our system is to list the photographer first
separated by a slash from the name of the individual who now owns the negative, or
the owner of the print collection. To avoid too much repetition, we do not always
credit collections of prints held by the editors where we have a named photographer.

In many cases we just do not know who took the photograph. For instance,
the Duncan collection of negatives which Ships in Focus bought in part some years
ago was obviously amassed not only through Duncan's own photography but also
through swopping negatives with others around the world, and there is rarely any
record of who took each negative. These are simply credited 'Ships in Focus'. Some
serial photographers (and we think of Tom Rayner especially) were in the habit of
taking multiple images of a ship and then swapping them with others. It is amusing
when selecting pictures to realise that one can have several images of a particular
ship on what is clearly the same occasion, but taken just a few feet apart! Where the
photographer or negative owner has neglected to put a name on the back of a print, the
credit is simply to the collection.

The subject of photographs leads us on to the question of digital images.
We much prefer to be lent images in order to get the scanning done ourselves, but
appreciate that some collectors and photographers prefer to do their own. We do
accept scans done on top-end equipment, and ask those using it to select at least 300
dpi, jpeg format, use the greyscale setting and to scan the images to a target size of 7 x 5
inches.

In this issue we include an index to the latest 'volume' of 'Record', which
we define as issues 41 to 44. We have also provided the usual 16-page 'bonus' section,
devoted to colour photographs. These are largely the work of Nigel Jones and Paul
Boot, to whom we offer our grateful thanks.

John Clarkson   Roy Fenton

November 2009

Shell Mex 1 arriving at Preston (see page 231). *[Roy Fenton collection]*

Fleet in Focus

THE LAST BIBBY LINERS

Roy Fenton and Adam Scott Gray

'Record'12 and 13 celebrated the four-masted ships owned by Bibby, and here the story of the company's liner and troopship tonnage is completed, up to the time the company moved to purely bulk-carrying ships.

Bibby have been consistent in applying to their ships the names of English counties suffixed by 'shire',

leaving others to use those of Scottish, Welsh and Irish counties, and indeed non-shire names from England. Interestingly, the company's more recent expansion into gas and bulk carriers required the use of several names not used before, including *Berkshire*, *Hampshire Lincolnshire* and *Wiltshire*.

DORSETSHIRE (1)

Harland and Wolff Ltd., Belfast, 1920; 7,445gt, 450 feet
Two Burmeister & Wain-type 6-cyl. 4SCSA oil engines by Harland and Wolff Ltd., Belfast driving twin screws.
Amongst a succession of elegant, four-masted ships built for Bibby, *Dorsetshire* (above) and her sister *Somersetshire* stood out for their functional ugliness. Their design was a compromise, as they were to be initially employed as ore carriers, with the possibility that they could be converted to troop carriers, and so were given unusually deep 'tween deck clearances. Even before they were delivered, the tin ore mined in Burma had begun to be smelted locally, so the pair were used on normal cargo services from the UK to India and Burma. They were not lacking in technical interest, however, as *Dorsetshire* was the largest motor ship yet built.

Conversion to a troop ship came in 1927, the work being carried out at Barrow-in-Furness (lower photograph, this page).

In 1939, *Dorsetshire* was converted to a hospital ship, and one wonders why she was chosen for this, as she might have been better employed trooping whilst

other passenger ships were turned into hospital ships. In this role she was attacked several times in the Mediterranean.

The left hand photograph at the top of the page opposite shows her trooping post-war, after various modifications which reduced her complement of troops and of boats.

In 1948 came yet another conversion, this time into an emigrant ship, her normal route being to Australia. The end of her career saw

a brief return to trooping during the Korean War, *Dorsetshire* making one voyage out from Liverpool in May 1953 and being laid up on her return in August. The right hand topmost photograph of *Dorsetshire* on the opposite page is dated 1954 and may well show her sailing from Liverpool for Newport where she arrived early in February to be broken up by John Cashmore Ltd. *[Roy Fenton collection (3); John McRoberts/J. and M. Clarkson]*

202

SOMERSETSHIRE (1)
Harland and Wolff Ltd., Belfast, 1921;
7,456gt, 450 feet
Two Burmeister & Wain-type 6-cyl. 4SCSA
oil engines by Harland and Wolff Ltd.,
Belfast driving twin screws.
Somersetshire had a career in almost
all respects identical to that of her sister
Dorsetshire, with cargo carrying followed
by trooping (as seen immediately above
on 16th September 1934), conversion to
a hospital ship and finally emigrant work.
War service as a hospital ship (right) also
saw her attacked, and indeed she was
lucky to survive torpedoing by *U 453* in the
Mediterranean in April 1942. Fortunately
there were no patients on board, but seven
members of her crew and hospital staff
were killed. She was abandoned but was
reboarded and limped into Alexandria.

Somersetshire is seen again (above left) as a hospital ship at Port Sudan in 1946 where she was waiting to embark wounded and disabled from the French *Chantilly* (9,986/1923).

Post-war service as an Australian emigrant ship was interrupted briefly by further trooping to East Africa during the operations against the Mau Mau in Kenya. By now she had a black

hull (above right, off Suez in 1951). *Somersetshire* was broken up by T.W. Ward Ltd. at Barrow-in-Furness during 1954. *[J. and M. Clarkson; Ships in Focus (2); J. and M. Clarkson collection]*

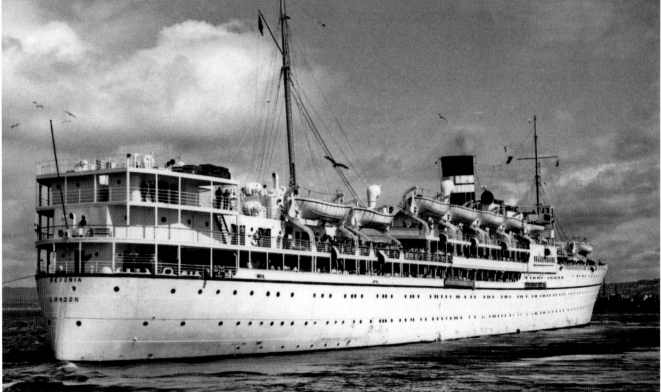

DEVONSHIRE (1)

Fairfield Shipbuilding and Engineering Co. Ltd., Glasgow, 1939; 11,275gt, 517 feet

Two 8-cyl. 2SCSA oil engines by Sulzer Brothers Ltd., Winterthur, Switzerland driving twin screws.

Like many older Bibby ships, *Devonshire* had several distinctly different careers. She was built as a permanent troopship, just in time for the Second World War, in which she served with distinction, her record including work as an infantry landing ship at Sicily, Salerno and in Normandy.

Trooping to Korea and Malaya continued after the war, and the largely grey livery seen in the middle photograph opposite was in use at this time. Like other troopers she was extensively rebuilt post war, going back to her builders in 1953 and emerging as seen in the bottom photograph on the page opposite and upper one on this page, the latter taken at Liverpool on 28th April 1956.

In this form she saw out troop carrying by sea.

Despite her 23 years, *Devonshire* then found a new role. Sold to British India who, like Bibby, were deeply involved with trooping and had surplus ships when this stopped in 1962, she was converted to an educational cruise ship and renamed *Devonia* (lower photo). She was broken up at La Spezia in 1967. *[Roy Fenton collection (2); F.W. Hawks; J. and M. Clarkson]*

HEREFORDSHIRE (2)

Barclay, Curle and Co. Ltd., Glasgow, 1944; 8,398gt, 493 feet
Two 4-cyl. 2SCSA oil engines by Barclay, Curle and Co. Ltd., Glasgow driving twin screws

Almost a quarter century after ordering *Dorsetshire*, Bibby again had the idea of building a cargo ship which could be converted for passenger carrying if trade warranted it. The result was another somehat incomplete looking ship (top photograph, taken in the Mersey on 19th February 1949). *Herefordshire* proved very useful, however, and was the only ship available to reopen the service from Liverpool to Rangoon whilst other Bibby liners were reconverted after war service.

In the event conversion was not necessary, and indeed she seems to have become surplus to Bibby's requirements even as a cargo ship. The upper middle photograph shows her on charter to Clan Line. In 1954 she began a seven-year charter to Port Line as *Port Hardy* (lower middle photograph). She returned to Bibby as *Herefordshire* in 1964, remaining with them until sold in 1969. Her new owners, Troodos, may have been aware of the intention to convert her for passenger carrying, as in 1971 they set out to fit her for cruising, having given her the rather trivial name *Merryland* (bottom). The project was abandoned, however, and after further service as a cargo ship she arrived at Kaohsiung for demolition in February 1973. *[John McRoberts/J. and M. Clarkson; J. and M. Clarkson collection (2); Airfoto of Malacca/J. and M. Clarkson]*

WARWICKSHIRE (2)

Fairfield Shipbuilding and Engineering Co. Ltd., Glasgow, 1948; 8,903gt, 498 feet

Steam turbines by the Fairfield Shipbuilding and Engineering Co. Ltd., Glasgow

With Bibby having specified oil engines since 1920, the return to turbines for the sisters *Warwickshire* (above and middle) and *Leicestershire* was surprising, but it did mean that the required speed of 15.5 knots could be achieved without the complication of twin screws. Building these ships with accommodation for 76 passengers was optimistic and, as independence for Burma drastically reduced the number of those wanting passage, *Leicestershire* became redundant and spent much of her time chartered to British India for their East African services. Indeed, it is perhaps surprising that this pair survived until 1965 in the Bibby fleet, and that such turbine-driven passenger ships could then still find buyers. They were subject to what would, in medical terms, be considered heroic surgery, being converted into passenger/car ferries for an overnight service between Piraeus and Crete. Renamed *Hania* (bottom), the former *Warwickshire* survived the 1966 bankruptcy of her owners, Typaldos

LEICESTERSHIRE (2)

Fairfield Shipbuilding and Engineering Co. Ltd., Glasgow, 1949; 8,908gt, 498 feet

Steam turbines by the Fairfield Shipbuilding and Engineering Co. Ltd., Glasgow

Sister to *Warwickshire*, *Leicestershire* spent part of her Bibby life on charter to British India. As the middle photograph shows, the charter involved painting up BI's funnel colours. She became the Greek car ferry *Heraklion* on her sale in 1965 (bottom), but her new life was to be short and tragic. On 8th December 1966 she was on a routine voyage from Piraeus to Crete when rolling in heavy seas resulted in vehicles on her car

OXFORDSHIRE (2)

Fairfield Shipbuilding and Engineering Co. Ltd., Glasgow, 1957; 20,386gt, 610 feet
Four steam turbines by the Fairfield Shipbuilding and Engineering Co. Ltd., Glasgow driving twin screws

Oxfordshire was the last of a long line of troopships, and resulted from a request made to Bibby by the British government in 1952. But British yards were busy, probably for the last time, and by 1957, when Oxfordshire was completed, there were changes afoot. National Service was ending, Britain was steadily withdrawing from East of Suez, and air liners now had the capacity to move troops in large numbers and quickly. Trooping by sea ended in 1962, and the upper photograph on this page taken at Southampton in July of that year probably shows Oxfordshire's last voyage. For her premature withdrawal the owners received considerable compensation from the taxpayer, the government having unwisely signed a 20-year charter agreement.

A new role was identified for her as an emigrant carrier, and Bibby chartered her to the Italian Sitmar organisation. But during conversion at Rotterdam, there

was a change of plan, and she was sold to Sitmar. Apparently, difficulties were foreseen over the agreement that Bibby's existing crewing arrangements would continue, with British officers and Indian ratings. When conversion work was completed in May 1964 she made her first voyage as Fairstar under the Liberian flag (bottom).

The emigrant trade eventually went the same way as troop carrying, and in 1973 Fairstar was further converted,

this time as a cruise ship, as which she mainly worked in the Far East. The Sitmar organisation was acquired by P&O in 1988 to become P&O Sitmar Cruises, but Fairstar survived this change, and the former troopship soldiered on, as it were, until 1997 when her 40-year old hull was broken up at Alang, India. A ship which had been something of an anachronism when built thus had a very long and useful life. *[J. and M. Clarkson collection; Airfoto of Malacca/J. and M. Clarkson]*

SHROPSHIRE (3)

Fairfield Shipbuilding and Engineering Co. Ltd., Glasgow, 1959; 7,244gt, 491 feet Doxford-type 6-cyl. 2SCSA oil engine by Fairfield Shipbuilding and Engineering Co. Ltd., Glasgow

The single-screw *Shropshire* (top) and her sisters *Cheshire* and *Yorkshire* were the first cargo ships Bibby had ordered which were not expected to be converted to passenger ships. Well aware that their Burmese services were in terminal decline, the company had an eye to chartering them out, and specified a service speed of 15.5 knots for these motor ships. A comprehensive outfit of derricks for general cargo work gave 50-ton and 20-ton lifts, plus a range from 12-tons to 5-tons. The middle photograph shows her on charter to Ellerman Lines in 1961.

    Shropshire was sold in 1972, Greek owners renaming her, first *Argiro* as seen bottom in May 1975, and after 1984 *Naftilos,* although she spent much of the 1980s idle at Piraeus. She completed one more voyage in 1985, to Chittagong where she was broken up. *[W.D. Harris; Tom Rayner; J. and M. Clarkson collection]*

CHESHIRE (3)

Cammell Laird (Shipbuilders and Engineers). Ltd., Birkenhead; 1959; 7,201gt, 491 feet

Doxford-type 6-cyl. 2SCSA oil engine by Fairfield Shipbuilding and Engineering Co. Ltd., Glasgow

Second of the trio was given the traditional Bibby name *Cheshire*, highly appropriate as her birthplace was in that county. She was, in fact, the first ship Bibby had ordered from an English yard since the company's rebirth in 1889. As the second photo shows, she spent time on charter, this shot showing her carrying Ellerman's funnel colours.

Cheshire was to be one of Bibby's shortest-lived ships, sold after just nine years to Messageries Maritime who renamed her *Mozambique*. After eight years on the French company's services to East Africa, she was sold on to Pacific International Lines of Singapore who renamed her *Kota Mewah* (bottom). She was broken up at Kaohsiung in 1984. *[J.K. Byass; Roy Fenton collection (2)]*

211

YORKSHIRE (3)

Fairfield Shipbuilding and Engineering Co. Ltd., Glasgow, 1960; 7,218gt, 491 feet Doxford-type 6-cyl. 2SCSA oil engine by Fairfield Shipbuilding and Engineering Co. Ltd., Glasgow

The upper photograph dates from 1966 and shows *Yorkshire* at a rocky, but so far unidentified location.

All three sister of this group were chartered out from time to time, but only *Yorkshire* was actually renamed, becoming *Eastern Princess* for Indo-China Steam Navigation Co. Ltd. from 1963 to 1964. She was photographed at Hobart on 8th February 1964 (bottom).

Yorkshire's departure from the fleet was also early, sold in 1971 as *Bordabekoa*. New owner Ramon de la Sota was Spanish (although he may well have thought of himself as a Basque), moving to flags-of-convenience in the years after the Spanish Civil War. In 1981 the ship was sold again, becoming *Sea Reliance*, and as such was broken up at Bombay in 1984.
[J. and M. Clarkson; Roy Fenton collection; David Kirby/Russell Priest collection]

LANCASHIRE (3)

Fairfield Shipbuilding and Engineering Co. Ltd., Glasgow, 1963; 9,210gt, 465 feet Sulzer-type 6-cyl. 2SCSA oil engine by Fairfield-Rowan Ltd., Glasgow
Lancashire was a development of the previous class, with a Sulzer engine and a slightly shorter hull. She had extra kingposts right aft for the derrick serving number 5 hatch, but without a 20-ton derrick. Her Bibby career was short, but after her sale in 1970 she spent a creditable 23 years with Pan-Islamic Steamship Company of Karachi as *Safina-e-Haider* before she was broken up at Gadani Beach in 1993. She featured under both names in 'Record' 36, page 227. [Airfoto of Malacca]

GLOUCESTERSHIRE (2)

Vickers-Armstrongs Ltd., Newcastle-upon-Tyne, 1950; 8,827gt, 471 feet Doxford-type 6-cyl. 2SCSA oil engine by Vickers-Armstrongs Ltd., Barrow-in-Furness
Bibby's policy of chartering out their newer ships was obviously successful, as when *Warwickshire* and *Leicestershire* were retired Bibby needed further ships, and acquired two ageing Prince Line ships to replace them. The ship that became *Gloucestershire* in 1964 was featured under this name and as *Cingalese Prince* and *Gallic* in 'Record' 43, and it is sufficient here to feature two further views of her (right) and to note that, following sale in 1971, she had a short career as *Cresco* before being broken up at Whampoa, China in 1972. [FotoFlite incorporating Skyfotos; V.H. Young and L.A. Sawyer]

STAFFORDSHIRE (3)

Vickers-Armstrongs Ltd., Newcastle-upon-Tyne, 1950; 8,807gt, 471 feet
Doxford-type 6-cyl. 2SCSA oil engine by Vickers-Armstrongs Ltd., Barrow-in-Furness

This ship also appeared in 'Record' 43 as *Bardic, Eastern Prince* and *Staffordshire*. Following engine damage in 1971, repairs were considered not worthwhile, and she was broken up in Hong Kong. *[J. and M. Clarkson]*

WORCESTERSHIRE (2)

William Doxford and Sons (Shipbuilders), Ltd., Sunderland, 1965; 10,040gt, 507 feet.
Sulzer-type 7-cyl. 2SCSA oil engine by George Clark and North Eastern Marine Ltd., Wallsend

Worcestershire and her sister *Derbyshire* were essentially enlarged versions of *Lancashire* but lacked the aftermost kingposts and had a taller, more boxed in superstructure (middle photograph). Like *Lancashire*, they had Sulzer machinery, despite being built by Doxford, renowned engine builders who had supplied Bibby for some years. In response to what they saw as threats from other engine builders, notably Sulzer and Burmeister & Wain, Doxford had hurriedly developed their 'P-type' engine, first produced in early 1960. But this engine had given some

problems, and Bibby were loath to use it, specifying a Sulzer instead. In the face of a declining order book, Doxford had changed their policy, and were now willing to fit other manufacturers' machinery into the hulls they built.

On disposal in 1976, *Worcestershire* went to one of Sir Ramon de la Sota's Liberian companies as *Bordagain* (bottom), finishing with Greek owners from 1982 to 1985 as *Katrinamar*. Indian breakers demolished her in 1985. *[J. and M. Clarkson (2)]*

DERBYSHIRE (3)

William Doxford and Sons (Shipbuilders) Ltd., Sunderland, 1965; 7,412gt, 507 feet.
Sulzer-type 7-cyl. 2SCSA oil engine by George Clark and North Eastern Marine Engineering Co. Ltd., Wallsend
Derbyshire is seen at two stages of her career: with Bibby (top) and as *Captain Lygnos* (upper middle). She went on to become *Chrysovalandrou* as which she almost cheated the breakers, abandoned by her crew when her engine room caught fire whilst anchored off Cartagena, Spain in November 1981. Burnt out but still afloat, she was towed into port and broken up. *[V.H. Young/J. and M. Clarkson; Roy Fenton collection]*

TORONTO CITY

Doxford and Sunderland Shipbuilding and Engineering Co. Ltd., Sunderland, 1966; 7,643g, 465 feet
Sulzer-type 6-cyl. 2SCSA oil engine by George Clark and North Eastern Marine Engineering Co. Ltd., Wallsend.
Previous post-war Bibby ships had been built with a view to chartering them out but, whilst built for charter, *Toronto City* and *Coventry City* were designed to meet the particular needs of one client, the Bristol City Line. Hence they did not just develop from earlier tonnage (although they followed Bibby's preference for Sulzer engines), but incorporated many refinements to meet the needs of the Bristol company's North Atlantic services. These included ice strengthening, refrigerated cargo lockers, and tanks for carrying chemicals. Controllable pitch propellers were operated from the bridge, and cargo equipment included deck cranes and two Hallen derricks in addition to some conventional derricks. *[P. Ransome-Wallis/Roy Fenton collection]*

COVENTRY CITY
Doxford and Sunderland Shipbuilding and Engineering Co. Ltd., Sunderland, 1966; 7,643g, 465 feet
Sulzer-type 6-cyl. 2SCSA oil engine by Fairfield, Rowan Ltd., Glasgow.
Histories of *Toronto City* and *Coventry City* appeared in 'Record' 33, so suffice it to say that, despite their having been built for a 20-year charter to Bristol City Line, they stayed for just eight years. By 1974, the relationship between Bristol City and Bibby had developed to the extent that the latter had taken over the former, so presumably penalty payments for premature termination were not arduous. Indeed, it seems that Bristol City sub-chartered the ships, and they were both photographed in charterer's colours. *Toronto City* was running for the Skandinaviske West-Africa Line of Bergen when photographed (page 215). She had four further names and was broken up in India during 1985; *Coventry City* carrying three further names and lasting a little longer, until the last day of December 1986 when she made her final call, this time at Kaohsiung. The photograph above was taken in March 1977. *[Roy Fenton collection (3)]*

WARWICKSHIRE (3)
Doxford and Sunderland Shipbuilding and Engineering Co. Ltd., Sunderland, 1967; 7,848gt, 528 feet
Doxford-type 6-cyl. 2SCSA oil engine by Hawthorn Leslie (Engineers) Ltd., Newcastle-upon-Tyne
An enlarged *Worcestershire*, *Warwickshire* saw a reversion to a Doxford-type engine, with the development of the 'J-type'. It was evidently successful, as these engines were fitted to several subsequent Bibby ships.

The 16-knot *Warwickshire* spent much of her life with the company under charter, including a period in the 1970s as *Arya Bod* for Iranian owners. After sale in 1980, she had a relatively short life before being broken up in China during 1985, but in that time managed three further names: *Furama, Sea Dragon,* and *Dragon Hill*. *[J.K. Byass]*

HEREFORDSHIRE (3)

Doxford and Sunderland Shipbuilding and Engineering Co. Ltd., Sunderland, 1972; 7,463gt, 530 feet
6-cyl. 2SCSA oil engine by Doxford and Sunderland Shipbuilding and Engineering Co. Ltd., Sunderland

Although Bibby began ordering bulk carriers in 1965, they still retained an interest in conventional cargo ships, taking delivery of a final pair in 1982, once again for time charter. *Herefordshire* and *Lancashire* followed the contemporary trend to move the superstructure well aft, although they were not unattractive vessels, at least compared with the bulkers and gas carriers which followed. They shared a layout with ships being built at the same yard for Bank Line (see 'Record' 18), but had a 50-ton Stülcken derrick to serve the two midships holds. These holds were fitted with twin hatches to facilitate the carriage of containers, as the above photograph shows.

In 1982 both were sold, *Herefordshire* becoming successively *Texas* and *Brooklyn*. In 1986 an engine fire cut short her career, and after being towed into Karachi in March *Brooklyn* was declared beyond economical repair and broken up at Gadani Beach. *[Fotoflite incorporating Skyfotos]*

LANCASHIRE (4)

Doxford and Sunderland Shipbuilding and Engineering Co. Ltd., Sunderland, 1972; 7,463gt, 530 feet
6-cyl. 2SCSA oil engine by Doxford and Sunderland Shipbuilding and Engineering Co. Ltd., Sunderland

Lancashire and *Herefordshire* had the melancholy distinction of being Bibby's last recognisable cargo liners, sold in 1982 when the fleet otherwise comprised bulk carriers and gas tankers. Indeed, under subsequent names *Virginia*, *Antibes* and *Amer Asha*, the former *Lancashire* was the last conventional Bibby ship to survive, not being broken up until 1998. The above photograph shows *Lancashire* on the River Scheldt on 14th July 1974. *[J. and M. Clarkson]*

EMPIRE PRIDE

Barclay, Curle and Co. Ltd., Glasgow, 1941; 8,418gt, 495 feet
Two 4-cyl. 2SCSA oil engines by Barclay, Curle and Co. Ltd., Glasgow driving twin screws

Fleet in Focus features usually ignore ships managed in wartime as not necessarily being representative of a company's design policy. However, an exception is being made for *Empire Pride* because of the interest of her design and her lengthy management by Bibby (top photograph). Laid down as a conventional cargo ship, she was turned into a troop carrier whilst building, with a capacity for a massive 2,200 men. After the war she continued in the ownership of the Ministry of Transport with Bibby as managers with her capacity reduced to what was probably a still very crowded 1,600. In 1954 she was replaced by *Devonshire* and sale to the Chandris organisation followed. She was taken to Lübeck for conversion, but sources differ on whether the ship that emerged as *Charlton Pride* was a pure cargo ship or an emigrant carrier. Chandris had some experience with emigrant ships, and may well have intended *Charlton Pride* to have been so used, but Anthony Cooke in his 'Emigrant Ships' maintains that she became a fast cargo liner, and Mitchell and Sawyer's 'The Empire Ships' supports this. Unfortunately photographs which could confirm this have proved elusive: can any reader help?

Just two years later in 1956 *Charlton Pride* was bought by Donaldson Line Ltd. and as *Calgaria* certainly was employed as a pure cargo liner with accommodation for just 12 passengers (lower photograph). In April 1963 she was renamed *Embassy* for a single loaded voyage to Hong Kong and the breakers. *[Roy Fenton collection (2)]*

NIGERIAN NATIONAL SHIPPING LINE:
A personal postscript by John Goble

Andrew Huckett's history of the Nigerian National Shipping Line Ltd. (NNSL) in the two previous issues of 'Record' has been especially enjoyable and interesting for me. The pictures accompanying his account took me back to the early summer of 1973 when I went along to the Merchant Navy Establishment (MNE) office (the 'Pool') near Liverpool's Pier Head looking for a ship. I had been applying for some shoreside employment without success as the increasing lengths of voyages and decreasing prospects of promotion were disillusioning me after 15 years in the industry. So my need for some coasting work that would finance me whilst I tried to find another career seemed to be met when I was asked to go along and meet a representative of NNSL on the *Dan Fodio*, laid-by in Hornby Dock for some voyage repairs.

I knew the West African trade well, had sailed with Nigerians frequently and found the prospect of just going around the land with ships, as needed, to be ideal for my purpose. The wages were much lower than I expected but a sufficient reward for not being too far from home. My attractiveness to my new employers, it soon became apparent, would be my reliability. Stevedores and others with business aboard NNSL ships were complaining that nobody in authority was ever apparent or available whilst the ships were in port. The company had three or four retired British masters on the payroll but they needed further support since most Nigerian officers found themselves too busy with their 'business' or social activities to attend to any shipboard duties.

The *Dan Fodio* was perhaps the best of the mixed bag of ships that formed the original fleet of NNSL. My quarters were especially spacious and included a bathroom with a proper bath that could be filled with fresh water as opposed to salt. I had only been aboard for a couple of days, however, when I was aroused at an early hour by the Bosun complaining that 'we get no fire in de wire' in their accommodation. This meant no electrical power aft. The duty engineer, who had also been put on the shake, could find no explanation at the main switchboard. It was only later, when the repair gangs boarded, that the cause became readily apparent. In such an elderly ship, all electrical power aft was distributed by a substantial copper cable that ran the length of the shelter deck. Local entrepreneurs, noticing the global copper shortage that year, had helped themselves to what must have been several hundredweight of the metal. My later experience would lead me to suspect a degree of inside help.

The other bought-in ships dating from the company's foundation were all beginning to show substantial wear and tear. The worst of the lot was the *King Jaja*, surprisingly the only ex-'liner' vessel, which generated amounts of funnel smoke that had the port authorities more or less permanently issuing penalty notices. Even the four 'River' class ships, barely four years old, were beginning to show signs of a lack of care and maintenance that caused endless problems in port with hatch coverings and cargo running gear.

On the morning of New Year's Day 1974 I drove down to Liverpool's Canada Dock to relieve the Mate on the *River Ethiope* but he had disappeared some hours previously. This vessel was, in effect, the flagship of NNSL as she maintained the so-called 'Lagos Express Service' alongside the *Fourah Bay* of Elder Dempster and the *Lagos Palm* of Palm Line. This was a cargo replacement service for the 'mail boats' which formerly sailed from the Mersey, the last of which, the *Aureol*, was now based in Southampton. It was Liverpool to Lagos direct and then back to Liverpool on a six-week cycle so I happily accepted an offer to go deep-sea again, with suitably increased pay,

Dan Fodio was the first Nigerian National ship which John Goble joined, and he describes it as 'the best of the mixed bag of ships that formed the original fleet of NNSL'. He recalled her as a classic 'open' shelterdeck ship where one could walk the length of the 'tweendeck as one huge space. She was very popular with the Nigerian crew as her generous boat deck allowed them to garage a fair number of second-hand cars. *[Roy Fenton collection]*

The boat deck of *King Jaja* could easily accommodate some half-dozen second-hand Peugeot estate cars. *[J. and M. Clarkson collection]*

and duly signed a six-month running agreement when we reached Lagos. The Master, Chief Engineer and Electrician were all British so it was obvious that NNSL wanted to keep reliable people in the key posts on this prestige service.

I soon found that my predecessor had left quite a few loose ends that explained his sharp exit but I also found that I had an excellent Nigerian bosun and carpenter who took pride in their ship. They were, nevertheless, as eager traders as just about everybody else on board so I decided to get these private freight arrangements sorted out from the start. I broke out a set of new padlocks and applied them to all the various lockers in the forecastle, poop and on the boat deck. I then collected the existing locks and their keys and explained to the other deck officers and the deck crowd that I was now in charge of who stowed what and where. My share of their freight would be in the form of a guarantee of their co-operation on passage. This was readily accepted as, after all, I would not be allocating the lion's share of the space to myself, neither would I, as a non-Nigerian, be expected to have any particular prejudices or loyalties that would show themselves as favouritism.

I did not have any control, of course, over the engineers or the stewards. I knew that cars were a most attractive item for private traders at that time. Whereas the bathroom on the *King Jaja* was attractive to me, the boat deck was any Nigerian mate's pride and joy as it could easily accommodate some half-dozen second-hand Peugeot estate cars, the premium brand for Nigeria's rugged roads. The boat deck space on the *River Ethiope* was a lot smaller but I was horrified one Sunday morning to return to the ship and find a small car neatly parked on each side. The proprietor of these vehicles turned out to be the Chief Steward who had tipped the crane driver who had loaded the catering stores the previous day to do a couple of additional lifts. Despite dire warnings from the former, who told me that he was both the agent and a relative of 'big men' in the company, I got someone in authority from the Liverpool office of NNSL to tell the Chief Steward that his 'protection' was not that powerful and that the offending vehicles would

now be removed at his expense. Watching the removal operation, I was quite happy to see a small dent put in the door of one car as a symbolic restitution for all the 'palaver'.

At least we could still have launched the lifeboats but I was a lot more annoyed when one pre-sailing inspection revealed a handsome four-seater leather settee stowed upright in the tunnel escape compartment in the poop house. 'How', I angrily demanded of the junior engineer whose cargo it was, 'the hell would you and your mates escape an engine room fire?' When the Chief learned about this escapade, you just knew who would be doing a lot of additional dirty jobs on passage. And what of the settee? It had to take its chance out on the open deck at first but I later came across it in one of the empty passenger cabins, a space in the gift of the Purser who doubtless made sure it paid a fat fare.

These cabins were not always available to the Purser as we did take passengers on occasion. The Nigerian Government was pressuring its citizens, who had been sent abroad at independence to study, to return home and work as directed for their country. I felt sorry for many of these Nigerians because this forced repatriation meant that they brought wives who were often British and teenage children, equally British, back to a world that would be both alien and a lot less comfortable. Their growing dismay as the ship sailed south into the heat of West Africa and their first sight of the shambles that was Apapa Quay as they disembarked were quite distressing to see.

The passenger accommodation was always empty going north but it certainly got a lot of use during the fortnight that we were in Nigeria. Every lunchtime the saloon was packed out with freeloaders 'from de office' and then the afternoon was the time when several senior managers and their attractive 'secretaries' needed to lie down for an hour or two. My Second Mate also had a habit of finding his way into a spare cabin with the odd 'cousin' when he should have been tending the deck. My passkey soon smoked him out but I did often upset the odd 'business meeting' in other cabins in the course of my search, to the embarrassment of all concerned.

The very varied group of ships that Nigerian National started out with seemed to those in the West African trade as a very dull bunch in comparison with the smart new ships coming into service in Ghana's Black Star fleet. However, when NNSL did buy new, they acquired two equally attractive vessels, *Ahmadu Bello* (right) and *Nnamdi Azikiwe* (below). These were almost carbon copies of Palm Line's *Ibadan Palm* class, but, importantly, they had steel weatherdeck hatch covers which were a blessing in the rainy season when compared with Palm Line's stubborn insistence on sticking with hatchboards. *[J. and M. Clarkson; FotoFlite incorporating Skyfotos]*

Private trade on the northbound leg was a lot less attractive in terms of profit. Palm oil, yams, cassava and other culinary items yielded but small returns and were often just genuine gifts for expatriate friends and relations. Snails were a particular delicacy and I remember one officer running the shower cubicle in a spare cabin as a ranch for some giant specimens who climbed all over the bulkheads between dousings. Dried small prawns were another gourmet item but the smell of them meant that they were banned from the accommodation. More sinister items were moving north, of course, and the ship was a prime target for the Waterguard rummage teams in Liverpool who would descend on us en masse, old hands and trainees together.

We were such an obvious suspect that I doubt that anybody on board so much as tried to bring in any drugs. I do know that it was a darned nuisance to me as I always liked to bring a few cartons of cigarettes and the odd bottle of whisky over the odds. Luckily, the rummagers were gentlemanly enough never to actually search my quarters. It was a further nuisance in that I had to get the carpenter to dismantle the deckhead and bulkhead panels because at least that way it avoided damage to them by clumsy hands in Liverpool. It made the crew's communal quarters look a mess but, as the crew didn't seem to mind, eventually we left the panels off all voyage. There was one trip where the Master was asked by one of the senior managers in Apapa

to take some veneered shelf samples back to Liverpool 'for safe passage' and which would be collected by a 'prospective importer' there. One evening, sitting in his dayroom over a drink, he asked me to look at these items. They comprised a bundle of about half-a-dozen foot-long, inch-thick planks. They were very attractively finished in a good-quality mahogany veneer but the ends seemed rather crudely finished. After a couple more drinks, and now joined by the Chief Engineer and Electrician, we decided to have a closer look and prised off one end of one shelf. The interior looked like a plank of plain obeche as one might expect but we then decided to check the other end and found it had a partially hollowed centre. It looked to be empty. What should we do, we wondered over another glass or two? Options were discussed and eventually we decided to bung the lot overside. Nobody came looking for the curious cargo in Liverpool and the manager had left the company when we returned to Lagos. So it became just another yarn of West Coast life.

During autumn 1974 my monthly pay cheques started to arrive several days in arrears and this, I knew from friends already sailing under foreign flags, was always a good sign to be moving on. Harrisons of Liverpool were offering well-paid positions in their 'five-fathoms club', as their coastal relief officers were called by the deep-sea staff. So I joined their number at the end of the year but that, as all good seafarers say, is a story for another time.

A TALE OF TWO MISTLEYS
Douglas J. Lindsay

As related in 'Records' 41 to 43, W.N. Lindsay Ltd. was a grain trading firm, established in 1864 and flourishing under the same family's ownership to this day. In the mid-1920s it drifted into owning two small steam coasters, the *Castlerock* and the *Grosvenor*, which it used for moving its own grain cargoes, and in particular for transhipment of bagged barley from ocean-going ships. It subsequently disposed of the *Castlerock* in 1938 and sold the *Grosvenor* in 1943. In the meantime the steamer *Drumlough* had been acquired in 1937.

The two Mistleys

Douglas W.N. Lindsay of the owning family had always wanted to go to sea but had been prevented for complex dynastic reasons. His opportunity came with war in 1939 when he joined the *Drumlough* and served on her until the end of hostilities in 1945. The *Drumlough* had a remarkable war, serving as a supply ship for the fleet at Scapa and operating mainly on the east coast of the UK, but throughout the war was never touched by enemy action. Legend has it that on occasion she shipped whole cargoes of 15-inch shells from Portsmouth to Scapa.

In 1945 an unscathed Douglas W.N. Lindsay left the sea, rejoined the family business and took charge of the shipping department in tandem with its long-serving manager, J. Douglas Ormiston. He arrived full of ambition and with various new contacts for business for the family ships, but with only the *Drumlough* to serve them. He set about acquiring more ships with some vigour, hampered only by the company's unwillingness to spend very much on any one ship. This led to his becoming an expert in picking up elderly tonnage, operating it for a limited time then scrapping it if no other end had befallen it in the meantime.

The *Mistley* had been built in 1922 and registered at Harwich as No. 1 in 1923 for F.W. Horlock's Ocean Transport Co. Ltd. Horlocks were millers and grain merchants based at Mistley in Essex and as their biggest and best acquisition the ship's naming scheme is obvious. They also owned Thames barges. By the end of the war they had decided to dispose of the by now elderly *Mistley* and found a willing buyer

Photos of the first *Mistley* are scarce, but two are available: the first, slightly fuzzy, is believed to show her approaching Mistley quay in the 1930s. *[Douglas J. Lindsay collection]*

Mistley (1) alongside, possibly at Buckie: can anyone confirm his? *[Douglas J. Lindsay collection]*

in W.N. Lindsay. The bill of sale shows a purchase price of £10,500 – a not inconsiderable sum for an elderly steamer at that time. But she was known to have been kept in excellent condition so presumably carried a premium.

The *Mistley* (1) commenced trading for W.N. Lindsay on 9th January 1946 and for the first year of operating for her new owners traded almost exclusively between either the Tees or Blyth and London with coal, returning with scrap from London to the Tees. It is interesting to note that her cargo books show her operating on behalf of M.F. Horlock and Company, so it would appear she came with some form of cargo agreement. The books show a modest but steady profit: selecting voyage 33 at random, the ship earned £373.14.8d freight on 441.2 tons of coal from Blyth. She earned £7.5.2d demurrage, less brokers' commission of £9.10.6d and ship expenses of £227.8.2d, giving a profit of £144.1.2d. The following trip north with scrap to the Tees made a profit of £93.14.6d. When the Horlock cargoes finished at the end of January 1947, the ship showed cumulative earnings of £6,245.16.9d, and a cumulative profit of £1,048.3.2d

With the end of the Horlock business the ship entered two trades which were to be definitive for the company for some years to come. The first was bagged cement cargoes from the Thames to the north of Scotland, a trade introduced to it through the Hay and Co. connection. Until the end of the Second World War these cargoes had been fixed by the suppliers, but Hays then negotiated a deal to fix their cargoes themselves, and passed on the arrangement to W.N. Lindsay. The second trade involved short trips with coal from the north east of England and Fife ports to Leith, Granton and Grangemouth. Working south with 'open market' cargoes, the ship settled into a regular routine for the next couple of years.

Mistley continued in these North Sea trades, leading a quiet and blameless life. Occasional cargoes took her further afield, such as carrying potash from Hamburg to Ayr followed by barrels of Manx herrings from Peel to Cuxhaven then softwood from Hamburg to Llanelli to account of the National Softwood Broker, a government office.

The cargo of herrings had an interesting sequel. On 2nd September 1948 the *Mistley* loaded 2,632 barrels of herrings at seven shillings a barrel, this plus 'loading payable by shippers' gave earnings of £941.14.10 pence and a profit of £88.14.9d. The trip took almost exactly 12 days. Thirty years and one month later, on 28th September 1978, I fixed the *Roselyne* (2) for an identical cargo from Peel to Scheveningen. The freight earned was a lump sum of £3,125.00 for a profit of just over £500. Such is inflation. The voyage took ten days but the cargo book records laconically that the ship was 'delayed two and a half days - blown out of Peel.' Peel has an open pier and if the wind comes away from the north of west it becomes untenable.

In 1950 *Mistley*'s luck changed. She went aground on the north east coast in May but got off again without damage. On 3rd October 1950 she went aground while entering Berwick-on-Tweed with a cargo of bagged cement. Part of her cargo had to be offloaded into the *Lindean* (by now

owned by a subsidiary of George A. Morrison Ltd.). Again, she was got off without damage and sailed on the 5th for Blyth. But in the early hours of Friday 6th October she ran up the rocks at Embleton, Northumberland, in thick fog. The entire crew took to their lifeboat and were towed to safety by a passing coble.

When the fog lifted the next day the ship was found to be hard aground with a 45 degree list. A diver's inspection found her to be holed and flooded along most of her length, including the engine room, and on 10th October she was declared a constructive total loss and abandoned to underwriters. These worthies invited offers for the scrap 'as lies', and that was the end of the first *Mistley*.

This left W.N. Lindsay short of a ship so, in early 1951, they bought the steamer *Coe-Pam* built in 1920. The ownership of the *Coe-Pam* has caused some difficulties to historians over the years. She was never owned by S. William Coe and Co. Ltd. of Liverpool; this was just a coincidence of name. Registers suggest that a London river pilot named Ernest Coe owned her but my memory is different: I was there as a 10-year-old when W.N. Lindsay took her over, and I remember being terrified by a fierce teenage girl from, I think, Latvia. She was the daughter of the ship's actual owners who, if not Latvian, were certainly refugees from one of the Baltic states. This girl had survived the Second World War in Latvia and was tough (and fierce) in a way I could barely start to comprehend. The pilot, if there was such, must have been providing UK national cover for her real owners.

For some reason my father regarded the name *Mistley* as a lucky one, and it has to be said the first *Mistley* had operated very well until it all went wrong. Therefore the *Coe-Pam* was re-named *Mistley*, and operated in the W.N. Lindsay trades for some years. Photos of her are more plentiful thanks in part to a set of albums of W.N. Lindsay ships put together for the company by Captain Chris Reynolds in 1984. It is quite difficult to tell the two ships apart but two clues are that *Mistley* (1) had an extra set of big cowl ventilators on the aft end of the fiddley and a flat front to her (rather larger) wheelhouse. *Mistley* (2) only had a single pair of large ventilators at the fore end of the fiddley, to serve the stokehold, and had a gently curved front to her midships house with a smaller wheelhouse.

The *Mistley* (2) continued in W.N. Lindsay trades for some years, with a growing emphasis on cargoes to the Orkney Islands and, especially, to Shetland. Mostly she led a quiet life but, in an uncanny echo of the first *Mistley*'s change of fortune,

Mistley (2) in original condition as *Weston* (above), arriving at Preston in mid-1930s. She was always prone to listing. *[World Ship Society Ltd.]*
Mistley (2) as *Coe-Pam* (below) again at Preston. During the five years under this name, from 1947 to 1952, a *wh*eelhouse has been built on her bridge. This picture also shows the curved front to her 'midships house. *[J. and M. Clarkson]*

Mistley (2) heading up-channel about 1954. *[Fotoflite incorporating Skyfotos/Douglas J. Lindsay collection]*

in 1956 life became more dramatic. On Friday 16th March 1956 W.N. Lindsay's *Roselyne* (1) had an engine room explosion and was left drifting helplessly 45 miles north west of Rattray Head while on passage from Aberdeen to Belfast with a cargo of oats. *Roselyne* was W.N. Lindsay's first venture into motor ships, having been built in Holland in 1939, and bought by W.N. Lindsay in 1955. Both company and crew were struggling to come to terms with (to them) newfangled machinery. Chief engineer Joe Cowie (who was later a captain with the company – those kind of switches were nothing unusual) reported that he could not fix the engine so the *Mistley* was despatched from Dundee, where she was loading sand, to rescue the *Roselyne.*

Meantime the fishing vessel *Steadfast* had been standing by; the weather was bad and visibility poor. The *Roselyne* drifted towards the coast for 24 hours before managing to get an anchor down and lay rather precariously until the *Mistley* arrived and got a line on to the *Roselyne* at lunchtime on Sunday 18th. But it parted soon after and the *Steadfast* held the *Roselyne* off the coast until *Mistley* could reconnect the tow line. The convoy then set off and arrived in Buckie 40 hours later after an epic struggle. The captain of *Roselyne,* Jimmy Bruce, was the company's senior master and came from Buckpool, next to Buckie. The *Mistley's* master James Stewart (he had sailed with my father during the war) came from Portknockie, also next to Buckie, and

the *Steadfast's* skipper was also from Buckie. All three men had known each other since childhood. A rather fuzzy picture of the convoy arriving at Buckie is the only memento of a tricky feat of seamanship.

Throughout the life of W.N. Lindsay as ship owners the crews were with very few exceptions drawn from the Moray Firth area and the Northern Isles. Most stayed with the company for many years: some from before the Second World War, others like Captain James Stewart, had sailed with Douglas W.N. Lindsay during the war and remained with the company until he retired in 1965. Captain James Bruce was regarded as the commodore captain (not that there was anything formal about it, he was just a very strong personality seen as the leading captain of the fleet) and grew to be a personal friend of Douglas W.N. Lindsay as well as mentor to the young Douglas J. Lindsay. He was also with the firm for many years. A strong two-way relationship and loyalty existed between owners and the crews, and for many years the company was known as 'the Buckie Navy'. The Moray Firth crews were ex-fishermen; straightforward, often unqualified men but marvellous seamen: tough, able and scared of nothing except their own superstitions. Given the firm's operations in stormy northern waters, these men's abilities were a significant contribution to the success of the business. They took an intense pride in the appearance of their ships, and one of the few points of friction with the management was their constant demands for paint!

After the excitement of the *Roselyne* rescue, *Mistley* headed south to deliver her cargo of sand, and settled back into W.N. Lindsay's humdrum

Mistley tows *Roselyne* (1) into Buckie. Conditions were quieter by the time they arrived. *[Douglas J. Lindsay collection]*

trades. By the summer it had been decided to scrap the old lady and, for her last job before going to the knacker's yard, she was booked to do the annual Northern Lighthouse coal run. For many years W.N. Lindsay had a contract with the Northern Lights Commissioners to deliver a year's worth of coal round its lighthouses on the east side of Scotland and the northern isles. A general delivery to Fair Isle was always included in the contract. It involved the ship creeping close in under cliffs, cuddling up to isolated rocks and generally going places they didn't normally. The story of the Northern Lighthouse coal run is worth an article on its own.

In 1956 *Mistley* was selected for the job. She loaded at Blyth then worked her way, lighthouse by lighthouse, up to North Ronaldsay in the Orkneys. After this delivery, captain James Stewart misjudged the height of tide and his position while leaving for Fair Isle and the ship stranded on the Reefdyke at 5.30 pm on 19th June. The weather was calm and, with *Mistley's* decks awash, the crew took to their boat. They were taken in tow by Dr S. Peace, who was fishing nearby, and landed at the lighthouse pier they had so recently vacated.

The sad demise of the second *Mistley*. The photograph was taken at low water on 24th June 1956. Her remains can be seen at low water springs to this day. *[Douglas J. Lindsay collection]*

An insurance surveyor was sent from Glasgow to look at her and, after some difficulty getting aboard because of the exposed position, declared the ship a constructive total loss. She broke up quite quickly after that.

This was the end of Mistley as a ship's name with W N Lindsay, and nearly the end of steamers in the company. There was an odd little codicil to *Mistley's* loss. The underwriters paid out her full insured value and it was a good deal more than the scrap value she had just been sold for. Before going north she had been emptied of stores and generally reduced to minimum condition. All this prompted one of the national daily papers to run an article implying heavily that it might all have been deliberate. I recall my father apoplectically waving this under my nose and the firm took legal advice which was to the effect that yes, they might well have a case for libel, but that the costs and uncertainties made it a bit of gamble to pursue the matter. W.N. Lindsay not being gamblers by nature, the matter was dropped but was guaranteed to get my father going for years afterwards if the topic ever came up. Try as I might I have not been able to locate this article but the memory is too vividly imprinted to be false. It would be interesting to find it.

See also page 233 for a follow-up to the Lindsay story.

PUTTING THE RECORD STRAIGHT

Letters, additions, amendments and photographs relating to features in any issues of 'Record' are welcomed. Letters may be lightly edited. Communications by e-mail are quite acceptable, but senders are asked to include their postal address. Correspondence on subjects in multipart articles is usually held over until the series has been completed.

The editors would deem it a great kindness if readers submitting letters for this column would as far as possible follow our current editorial style, and in particular put names of ships into upper and lower case italics and not capitals.

Wirral revisited
Having read 'Record' 36 again I am intrigued by the coincidence of names in 'Tramping into Obscurity' Part 2. Tyson, Edgar Shipping Ltd. was closely followed by Wirral Shipping Co. Ltd. There was the Wirral Transport Co. Ltd. (J. Edgar and Co. Ltd. managers) of Liverpool which had ships named *Wirral*. The first was built in 1911 and was torpedoed and sunk in May 1917. The second was built in 1925 and was sold to the Alexander Shipping Co. Ltd. (Capper Alexander and Co., managers) in 1934. She was torpedoed and sunk in May 1943. Was there any connection between J. Edgar and Co. and Douglas Edgar of Tyson, Edgar Shipping Ltd. and between the latter company and

Wirral Shipping Co. Ltd.?
On the following page 205 there is a reference to the Bawtry Shipping Co. Ltd. This is the same company that bought the Elder Dempster Liner *Aba* that, under the name *Matrona*, capsized in Bidston Dock, Birkenhead in October 1947.
GEOFF HOLMES, 17 Bayswater Court, Newport Avenue, Wallasey, Cheshire CH45 8QJ

The coincidence of names is intriguing. However, the Wirral Shipping Co. Ltd. and its successor the Wirral Steamship Co. Ltd. were managed by a Henry Elmer, who was based in London. Ed.

On photographs
In 'Record' 43, page 174, the date of the photo HMS *Cuillin Sound* was probably 1st September 1946. The vessel had already been wrecked as *James Clunies* by 1st September 1949.
RICHARD PRYDE, 4 Portlight Close, Mistley, Manningtree, Essex CO11 1UD
Wrist duly smacked. Ed

The photograph of *Huta Sosnowiec* in the Kiel Canal in July 1969, on page 165 of 'Record' 43 and credited to John G.

The *Wirral* of 1925 was built by Lithgows Ltd., Port Glasgow for the Wirral Transport Co. Ltd. Sold to Capper, Alexander and Co. in 1934 and renamed *Holmbury*, she was torpedoed by *U 123* in the Atlantic on 5th May 1943. *[Warwick Foote]*

Callis, was my original work - the negative would have been exchanged.
MALCOLM CRANFIELD, 8 Foxcover Road, Heswall, Wirral L60 ITB

Odd erections

Alpha Zambesi − the odd erection on top of the bridge, visible in all three photos on page 184 of 'Record' 43, is the radar cabin housing the transmitter/receiver. At that time this equipment was quite large (and noisy when operating) so was usually mounted on top of the bridge (the radar display would, of course, have been in the wheelhouse). The mast of the radar scanner is mounted directly above the radar cabin. Later, in most ships, the radar transmitter/receiver was mounted internally. In some ships (some of the post-war Bank Line ships come to mind) it was mounted in the radio room itself – most inappropriately considering the noise produced by the radar. This must have made radio watch-keeping a bit of a nightmare when the radar was on – even when wearing headphones! *Doris Clunies*, on page 181, has exactly the same arrangement with a very tall scanner mast but, as *Eudoxia* on page 181, a much lower radar mast and different scanner.
DAVID WITTRIDGE, 25 Fairlawn Close, Rownhams, Southampton SO16 8DT

Alpha Zambezi page 184. I suggest the boxy structure on the monkey island is possibly a battery locker for the radio installation.
CAPTAIN JOHN ANDERSON, 523 Louise Road, Ladysmith, British Columbia, Canada V9G 1W7

Araluen nightmare

The photos of *Araluen* on page 194 of 'Record' 43 show a naval architect's nightmare. Lengthening a ship required long and laborious 'hand cranked' calculations in the old days, estimating the weights of the two halves, their centres of gravity and other factors, to ensure that the sections would be stable and float at a reasonable trim when the ship was cut in two. Heaven help it if, for instance, the combined weight calculated for the two halves did not add up to the total weight of the ship before it was cut in two! The stability calculations could be quite tricky, especially for the bow section, and I would have agreed with removing the foremast. In the last photo on page 195 this appears to have been done before the fore half was salvaged.
TONY SMYTHE, 35 Avondale Road, Rayleigh, Essex SS6 8NJ

More on MACs

A letter printed in the 'Navy' in November 1970 about the origin of the MAC ship concept is of interest and I have reproduced it in full.

'I was interested to read the account of the Merchant Aircraft Carrier in the October issue of 'Navy' and it might be of interest to your readers to have first-hand details of the birth of these ships.

In 1941 I was the Convoy Planning Officer in Trade Division of the Admiralty. It was clear that one of the means of reducing our appalling merchant ship losses was by affording each convoy its own air support, thereby hampering the concentration of U-boat packs. To this end the United States had promised us 27 escort carriers. Then came Pearl Harbour and it was obvious to me that those carriers would take a long time in arriving.

I was scratching my head over this one evening in my office when Sir Douglas Thomson, a director of Ben Line who was one of the excellent band of shipowners who performed liaison duties between the Ministry of Shipping and the Admiralty, came into my office and asked me why I was looking worried. I explained the problem and he said 'I have often wondered why, with ships that can carry grain which can be poured down a chute and sucked out the same way, it should not be possible to do away with cranes and derricks. You can then have a flat-top deck to operate aircraft.' This struck me as an excellent idea and there and then we called on Naval Air Division who poured cold water on the scheme, saying that a 12-knot ship was far too slow to operate Swordfish. I pointed out that the number of days in the North Atlantic when there was insufficient wind for a Swordfish to take off and land were few and far between. This produced no favourable reaction.

Unwilling to be thus rebuffed I made an appointment to see Sir James Lithgow, the Director of Merchant Ship Building, a day or so later. He was most cooperative and said he would do all he could to help. With the enthusiastic support of my director, Brian Schofield, a meeting was convened in the Admiralty attended by all the interested parties.

The Director of Naval Construction opened proceedings by saying it would take a year or more to design such a ship. Whereupon Sir James Lithgow, who was a great man, took an envelope out of his pocket and spoke roughly thus-wise: 'Here is the sketch design. I have two ships about to be built at Burntisland which can be converted without undue delay in their coming into service. I am prepared to do this provided I am not interfered with by the Admiralty.' Naval Air Division was won round, the scheme was approved by the Board and thus the Macship was born.

Incidentally, rumour had it that later on a Swordfish landed on its parent ship bow to stern, instead of the more orthodox method, when a following gale was blowing.'

G.N. Brewer, R.N. (retired)

DEREK ATHERTON, 3 Twyford Place, Fingerpost, St Helens, Merseyside WA9 1BN

I was mate of the *Scottish Star* in 1968 when she was incarcerated in the Suez Canal as a result of the Six-Day War of 1967. One of the 14 members of the Great Bitter Lakes Association was the Bulgarian vessel *Vassil Levsky* (not *Basil Levski*). Not air conditioned, of course, and it was rather hot out there, so they had rigged the long saloon table on the boat deck under a canvas awning, and her huge Bulgarian captain entertained there in considerable style. None of the Bulgars spoke English but that did not seem to matter after a few of their amazing ouzos. We knew she had been Turnbull Scott's *Saltersgate*. We (even her crew) thought that she had been one of the catapult-launched jobs – not the flat-top aircraft carrier your article shows her to have been as *Empire Mackendrick*.

Whilst I was there the Chief and other engineers of the *Port Invercargill* spent a lot of time and hard work putting *Vassil Levsky's* machinery to rights. Much of it was similar to that in many of the older Port liners so fixing it was, to them, a piece of cake.

We were like a big family out on the Lake. Despite language differences we all knew ships and were able and willing to help out on any ship which needed assistance. We were a merry mix of Americans, Swedes, West Germans, Czechoslovakians, Bulgarians, Poles, French and Commonwealth Brits. I was there four months and we never got ashore – did not particularly want to as war between the Egyptians and Israelis was raging

Scottish Star under repair at Hebburn, Tyneside on 7th July 1957 with a tank-cleaning vessel alongside. *[J. and M. Clarkson collection]*

all around us, especially on Saturday nights.
CAPTAIN A.W. KINGHORN, 15 Kendal Avenue, Cullercoats, North Shields, Tyne and Wear NE30 3AQ

'Caernarfonshire Sail': the author responds

John Naylon and others outside of Caernarfonshire and Wales are rightly permitted to say that 'Caernarfonshire Sail' is something of a puzzle. The key to the puzzle is clearly given in the first paragraph of the book's introduction - the main source for the book is 'Hen Longau Sir Gaernarfon' written in the vernacular by schoolmaster David Thomas, a National Eisteddfod winner of 1943, first published in 1952 and republished in 2008. The two appendixes of 'Hen Longau Sir Gaernarfon' list over 1,500 Caernarfonshire sailing vessels of different types - where built, builders, tonnage, figurehead type and short history. It is this wealth of data spanning 150 years that stimulated me to write 'Caernarfonshire Sail'. In fact, what I have attempted to do is to fill a gap, or provide a guide to sailing vessel types, and hope it is a worthy corollary to 'Hen Longau Sir Gaernarfon'. As Welsh readers of the original book will agree there is a paucity of information concerning the description of vessel types that David Thomas says he did not cover, admitting that he was inexperienced in shipboard matters and that he gathered his information concerning maritime Caernarfonshire purely by research and much conversation.

In the circumstances I make continual reference throughout my book to the source and the data analysis of the appendixes - hence the bewilderment experienced by John and others who are yet to read David Thomas's 'Hen Longau Sir Gaernarfon', soon to be published in English. Maybe it is a case of 'the cart before the horse' and if so I apologise.

'Caernarfonshire Sail' is good value at £9.50, especially to those youngsters to whom it is aimed, coming to the subject for the first time, and who have never known the beauty and glory of sail. I sincerely hope it will generate a zeal and enthusiasm that I have experienced myself during a lifetime of my own interest in sail.

As to the title, I am proud to say it was the choice of a young shipwright and competent sailing vessel master who believes in the future of sail. As a consequence I took the opportunity to write a plea for a sailing vessel for Wales and its youth, the same as in all maritime countries throughout the world, and trust that something will come of it.
OWEN.F.G. KILGOUR, Y Gorlan, 21 Meriadog Road, Colwyn Bay LL29 9NR

THE LAST VOYAGE OF *HEMSLEY-I*
Roy Fenton

Bunkering craft usually lead rather humdrum lives, pottering around ports and estuaries. One of the best known of these vessels in the Mersey in the 1960s was a quaint old craft, *Hemsley-I*, which was to have her moment of adventure, with more than a touch of farce.

Owners were Hemsley Bell Ltd. of Southampton who began business around 1932, or at least entered the register books by acquiring craft in that year, although there are reports that the founder was active in the First World War. Their first acquisition was modest, the small steam tug *Elsandra* (83/1903) which had been built at Falmouth. In 1934 came a more substantial craft, the former Admiralty oiler *Attendant*, which the company employed as a bunkering vessel at Southampton. It is assumed that the tugs *Elsandra* and later purchases *Fabia* (151/1919), *Marion* (46/1919) and *Talbot* (62/1913) were also used for bunkering work. They would be used to tow the company's ferro-concrete barges, including *Cretol* and *Cretoleum*, whose names suggest they carried fuel oil. The larger *Hemsley*, bought from Shell in 1936, was also suitable for this work.

In September 1939 *Attendant* was requisitioned by the Admiralty, and made her perilous way to Scapa Flow, presumably being used as a station oiler. The owners were not left bereft of tankers, however, as in 1944 they began to be given small ones to manage, including the 'Isles' class vessels *Empire Lundy* (288/1944) and *Empire Guernsey* (288/1945), the larger *Empire Tapley* (305/1944), and later the captured German-built *Empire Tigness* (407/1943).

Attendant returned to Southampton in 1945, and was to witness a period of expansion of the fleet, with two further Admiralty oilers of the numerous 'Creosol' class being purchased in 1947, *Scotol* and *Hickorol*. Mr Bell again applied his first name to them, so they became *Hemsley-I* and *Hemsley-II*. The latter worked in the north west of England, but was not retained long, being sold to Greek owners in 1950. *Attendant* soldiered on until 1964, mainly at Southampton, but was outlived by *Hemsley-I*, which became a familiar sight in Liverpool docks and the Manchester Ship Canal. At the advanced age of 53, and reputedly the oldest steamer on the British register, *Hemsley-I* was retired and sold to breakers in Antwerp in 1969. She was never to reach them.

Hemsley-I sailed from Liverpool on 10th May with a 12-man crew under Captain Kilby Lennard and proceeded southwards down the Irish Sea. At 12.45 am on 12th May *Hemsley-I* sent out a radio message that she was aground on Lizard Head, adding that she was 'underneath the light'. In response the Lizard lifeboat was launched, the German reefer *Parma* (3,932/1967) altered course and - scenting a salvage job - the Wijsmuller tug *Titan* (229/1956) proceeded towards this point on the south coast of Cornwall. Nothing was found, and so at 4.48 am the lifeboat at Sennen went out looking for the wreck. Meanwhile, the crew of *Hemsley-I* reported that they had left the vessel and were on rocks above high water level. It was only when they reached a house on the cliffs that they

A post-Second World War view of *Attendant* at anchor in the Solent in the company of a Short Sandringham. Two more flying boats can be seen in the distance. *[Roy Fenton collection]*

Hemsley-II at Preston in the late 1940s. Note the wood-panelled bridge front, and that she still carries the single mast with which these oilers were built. With her bridge so far forward, a pole was mounted on her bow to help the helmsman steer. *[Harry Stewart/J. and M. Clarkson]*

Hemsley-I sails from Eastham on 28th March 1968. As with *Attendant*, an extra mast has been fitted to support navigation lights and a radio aerial. *[Roy Fenton]*

found out where they really were: in Fox Cove, just above Porthcothan, on the *north* coast of Cornwall, on a stretch of coast that runs due north and south above Newquay. Clearly, in fog the *Hemsley-I* had turned east too early, and headed up the Bristol Channel and not as the crew thought the English Channel. The Sennen boat was recalled at 5.35 am after the master of *Hemsley-I* had reported that the crew were safe (three were taken to hospital with minor injuries or shock). The tug *Titan* quickly arrived, and the third lifeboat of the day, that from Padstow, was launched to stand by whilst attempts were made to tow *Hemsley-I* off the rocks, Captain Lennard having returned to the vessel. He signed Lloyd's Open Form agreement, but his ship's position was hopeless, with severe gashes in her hull. By 15th May 'Lloyd's List' reported that 'hopes of salvage were fading'.

Not only was this the end of *Hemsley-I* but, with her demise, Hemsley Bell Ltd. ceased ship owning.

Hemsley-I hard aground in Fox Cove, Cornwall. Despite the exposed position, it is reported that some scrap metal was extracted from the wreck. *[J. and M. Clarkson; Roy Fenton collection]*

Bunkering tankers of Hemsley Bell Ltd., Southampton

1. ATTENDANT 1934-1964
O.N. 136700 1,022g 584n
200.0 x 34.2 x 15.2 feet
T. 3-cyl. by H.M. Dockyard, Chatham;
700 NHP, 450 IHP, 8 knots.
5.7.1913: Launched by H.M. Dockyard, Chatham.
28.8.1914: Registered in the ownership of the Admiralty as the oiler ATTENDANT.
1926: In reserve at Rosyth.
27.9.1934: Acquired by Hemsley Bell Ltd., Southampton.
19.9.1939: Requisitioned by the Admiralty until 27.7.1945 and used at Scapa Flow.
10.1964: Sold to Lacmots Ltd., Queenborough for breaking up.
19.11.1964: Register closed.

Attendant. [J. and M. Clarkson collection]

2. HEMSLEY 1936-1947

O.N. 148719 927g 424n
190.0 x 32.7 x 13.2 feet
Oil engine by Werkspoor, Amsterdam, Netherlands; 442 BHP.
5.1915: Completed by Gebroeeder Pot, Bolnes, Netherlands (Yard No. 696) for N.V. Nederlandsche Indische Tankstoomboot Maatschappij, s'Gravenhage, Netherlands as LARA.
11.1.1926: Registered in the ownership of the Anglo-Saxon Petroleum Co. Ltd., London as SHELL MEX 1.
25.11.1936: Acquired by Hemsley Bell Ltd., Southampton, having recently been converted to a barge.
5.3.1937: Renamed HEMSLEY.
4.11.1947: Register closed on sale to France.

3. HEMSLEY-I 1947-1969

O.N. 139161 1,179g 567n
221.0 x 34.8 x 15.6 feet
T. 3-cyl. by John Dickinson and Sons Ltd., Sunderland; 141 NHP, 700 IHP, 9¼ knots.
23.6.1916: Launched by the Tyne Iron Shipbuilding Co. Ltd., Willingdon (Yard No. 205).
28.10.1916: Registered in the ownership of the Admiralty as the oiler SCOTOL.
11.1916: Completed.
15.7.1947: Transferred to the Ministry of Transport, London.
31.7.1947: Acquired by Hemsley Bell Ltd., Southampton.
7.11.1947: Renamed HEMSLEY-I.
1969: Sold to breakers in Antwerp.
12.5.1969: Wrecked during fog in Fox Cove, near Porthcothan, about six miles south of Padstow, whilst on a voyage from Liverpool to Antwerp in ballast.
13.8.1969: Register closed.

The Dutch-built bunkering tanker *Lara* (seen on the Kiel Canal) became *Shell Mex 1* (photographed at Preston) and was bought by Hemsley Bell Ltd. as a dumb barge and renamed *Hemsley*. [Willem Moojen; World Ship Society Ltd.]

The Admiralty oiler *Scotol*, seen here in 1919, became *Hemsley-I* in 1947. [National Maritime Museum N.4336]

4. HEMSLEY-II 1947-1950

O.N. 1342314 1,176g 451n
220.9 x 34.7 x 16.6 feet
T. 3-cyl. by J.G. Kincaid and Co. Ltd.,
Greenock; 85 NHP, 700 IHP, 9 knots.
30.11.1917: Launched by Archibald
McMillan and Sons Ltd., Dumbarton (Yard
No. 470).
25.2.1918: Registered in the ownership of
the Admiralty as the oiler HICKOROL.
3.1918: Completed.
23.9.1947: Transferred to the Ministry of
Transport, London.
31.12.1947: Acquired by Hemsley Bell Ltd.,
Southampton.
19.3.1948: Renamed HEMSLEY-II.
12.9.1950: Register closed on sale to N.T.
Papadatos, Piraeus, Greece and renamed
GRAMMOS.
1956: Sold to D'Alesio and Castaldi,
Livorno, Italy and renamed ARDENZA.
1967: Sold to Ottavio Novella, Genoa, Italy
and renamed PANNESI
1974: Transferred to Ciane-Arapo Cia. di
Nav. e Bunkeraggi S.p.A. (Ottavio Novella,
manager), Genoa.
9.1978: Broken up at La Spezia.

Hemsley-I off the Alfred Dock lock
entrance at Birkenhead (top) in the
middle 1960s. *[J. and M. Clarkson
collection]*
Still in Admiralty colours, *Hickorol*
arriving at Preston in pre-pylon days
(middle). *[Harry Stewart/
J. and M. Clarkson collection]*
Hemsley-II sailing from Preston with
pylons in the background, the ruination
of many photographs taken from the
Bull Nose (bottom). She carries an
early version of the funnel of Hemsley
Bell Ltd., simply black with a white
band. One of the port authority sand
pumps can be seen in the distance.
[World Ship Society Limited]

Hemsley-I approaches the locks at Eastham on a sunny 7th September 1967. She has the final, colourful version of the Hemsley Bell funnel: yellow with black top, and with blue letters HB on a white diamond edged with red. The editor, who took the photograph whilst still a student, is grateful to Paul Boot for restoring the 42-year-old Agfacolour slide to its original condition. *[Roy Fenton]*

LINDSAY FOLLOW-UP

I remember the *Blacksod* well, she arrived in St Helier Harbour during the winter of 1949/50 from Montrose with a cargo of potatoes. Always in my memory she really lived up to her name as being dark, drab and dirty. I have a photo of *Oranmore* in St Peter Port about the same time looking rather smarter. The caption on the photo of *John Evelyn* as *Maryston* referring to her loading coal for Guernsey is rather doubtful as I don't believe she ever visited Guernsey under that name: Dorey's always had the contract to carry all the various types of coal to our sister island.
DAVE HOCQUARD, Les Cotil des Pelles, Petit Port, St. Brelade, Jersey

Mention is made on page 42 of 'Record' 41 of Hay's schooner *Columbine* of Lerwick having been built in 1869. She was, in fact, built in 1834 at Cowes (by White?) and was registered at Lerwick on 19th August 1870 as port number 6 for Hay. The register was closed on 29th May 1913 with the vessel to be broken up. I think she was broken up due to old age rather than because there was a war on: after all, about 180 schooners and the like were to be casualties of war and were changing hands at astronomic prices. Several harbour hulks were put back under sail and a dozen or so luxury yachts were converted for carrying cargo.
MARTIN BENN, 2 Lonsdale Mews, Croston Road, Lostock Hall, Preston, Lancashire PR5 5NH
The author replies: My comment on page 42 did say 'bought' not 'built'. Quoting from the book 'Hay and Company – Merchants in Shetland' by James R. Nicholson, a Shetlander who had full access to the company records,

it says: 'Yet another important acquisition of this period [mid 1800s] was the schooner '*Columbine*' which arrived in September 1869 and was given a through overhaul at Freefield [Hay and Co's base] under the jurisdiction of Walter Colvin. It was said that he examined every bolt and treenail from the keel to the gunwale and refastened her throughout. In January, 1870 she was despatched with her first cargo for Hay and Co – a consignment of whale crang for a purchaser in Montrose.'

With regard to her demise, two forces were at work. Firstly, she was by then very old and in need of extensive restoration if she was to remain in service. The second, and perhaps more important, was that with the onset of the first war the fishing virtually ceased in Shetland and the Columbine's *primary reason for existing disappeared as there were no fish to carry away. Nicholson's book is a bit gnomic, saying on the one hand that a scarcity of shipping was causing the company problems in importing coal and other necessities, but also saying that '…on 10th August 1914 the company severed their own connection with shipowning when the old 'Columbine' was taken into dock to have her rigging removed. She was sold to Mr W.J. Sinclair, Bayview House, Hoswick, for £20 for breaking up and, in March 1915, she was towed to Hoswick by a vessel bearing her name – the Sumburgh motor packet 'Columbine''.*
No further explanation is given for what, on the surface of it, was an odd decision but there must have been powerful forces at work. I'm always interested in seeing other sources and information but Nicholson's book – the official history of the firm – is usually regarded as authoritative.

It was a pleasant surprise to see two pictures of ships in Shetland waters in 'Record' 41. To be exact, both were at Fair Isle, the island midway between Orkney and Shetland. The ships were photographed from exactly the same vantage point on a cliff top overlooking the North Haven, the island's harbour. *John Evelyn* is lying head to the north in this sheltered little deep-water inlet, moored by a line ashore from each quarter and an anchor out ahead. *Greenisland*, pictured with the camera pointing south, is moored in similar fashion – a line from her port quarter is clearly visible. On her port side is moored the island's mail boat *Good Shepherd* which, during winter, was hauled up the slipway on the beach in the background after each weekly trip to the Shetland mainland 22 miles distant.

A Fair Isle friend told me that the Northern Lighthouse Board supplied domestic coal once a year for the resident keepers and their families stationed at Fair Isle's two lighthouses – ten tons for each Principal Keeper and six tons for each Assistant Keeper; 44 tons in all. The Fair Isle residents also burned coal, so it became practice for a coaster taking a coal cargo north for Hay and Company in Lerwick to leave 100 tons aboard for delivery to Fair Isle on the way south. Before 1959 the coal was bagged aboard the ship at anchor there, and boated ashore in a communal effort of no little magnitude. I am also told that the furniture container aboard *John Evelyn* would most likely have held a schoolteacher's property, because the Northern Lighthouse Board used its own lighthouse tenders to move a keeper's effects between shore stations when he transferred between one lighthouse and another.

The photograph of *Karri* in 'Record' 42 neatly finishes off the sequence, for the North Pier in Fair Isle was completed in May 1959. As the photograph shows, the pier was long enough to allow the ship's forward half alongside, enabling coal to be discharged by grab into a truck. One can imagine the labour that was saved!
CHARLES SIMPSON, Wilhoul, Cunningsburgh, Shetland ZE2 9HG

The author replies: *I am obliged to Mr. Simpson for his corrections and further information, the only point I am unconvinced by is the suggestion that the contract to provide Fair Isle with its coal lay with Hay and Co: our records show that the Commissioners of Northern Lights through the Edinburgh coal merchant Bruce Lindsay (no connection, just a co-incidence of name) - chartered the ship from W.N. Lindsay. But Hays were certainly involved, right up to the final delivery each year at Muckle Flugga.*

I remember the sailing vessel *Penang* very vividly. My parents took me on a summer holiday to Edinburgh and Leith and with my father I visited Leith and Granton regularly and in my notebooks I listed all the ships in these busy ports. We were present shortly after the *Penang* berthed and I remember the awesome hush as spectators on the quay gazed at the tall masts and noted the yards and rigging. Your article gave the dates of her arrival as 1938 but I have newspaper cuttings of the vessel dated August 1937. The August 1937 'Sea Breezes' states that she sailed from Leith on 12th August 1937 for Madagascar. I think *Penang* was the last commercial sailing vessel to visit Leith.
SUTHERLAND MANSON, 6 Bower Court, Thurso, Caithness KW14 8JL

Regarding *Shetland Trader* (4) I can bring the story forward. In the twilight zone of Northern Cyprus I took a very hasty shot of her under the PRK flag and registered in Wonsan. It was some way out in Famagusta harbour and the shot was hasty because just along the Venetian walls there was a sentry box overlooking the North Cypriot military base with a man in it and I did not wish to become a statistic for fair trials abroad! Lloyd's Register came up with the identity as the name was unclear and not on their database at the time: they now have her switching to PRK March 2009 and taking the name *Blameless* in May 2009, although clearly both had happened by March 2009.
MARTIN WRIGHT via e-mail

Rosemarkie (1) of 1939 during her ten-year career with W.N. Lindsay. *[Douglas J. Lindsay collection]*

Two views (above and below left) taken in January 2009 of the *Roselyne* of 1955 abandoned in the Surinam River. Vegetation almost covers her and a bank has built up over her midships section leaving only the bow, with mast still standing, and stern showing. Her last recorded owners were in Anguilla, West Indies and she was deleted from 'Lloyd's Register' in 2000 as presumed broken up. *[Koos Goudriaan]*

Roseneath was the former British Electricity Authority collier *Poole Harbour* (above and below). *[Douglas J. Lindsay collection]*

The Bristol-owned and built *Hotwells* (above) was bought by W.N. Lindsay in 1970 and renamed *Rosewell*. *[Douglas J. Lindsay collection]*

TURKISH VETEREN STEAMERS

Nigel Jones

Many of Istanbul's fascinating steam ferries operated by Denizcilik Bankasi T.A.O. are featured in *Bosphorus Ferries,* 'Record' 28. This company also owned a substantial fleet of ocean-going steam passenger, passenger/cargo ships and, briefly, general cargo ships. Examples of each of these types were still in service well into the 1970s and early-1980s. Simultaneously, the few remaining privately owned Turkish-flag steam freighters were withdrawn from commercial use and dispatched to local breakers' yards; the last one in 1985. In common with several of the ferries, the oldest of these vessels was built prior to the First World War and, incredibly, lasted for over 60 years.

This tribute to the final era of Turkish veteran steamships' activity includes vessels constructed in Germany, Italy, Scandinavia, the United Kingdom and U.S.A. All were handsome vessels and, despite being mainly confined to trading locally in the Black or Mediterranean Seas during their twilight years, were a credit to their builders with an average life span of 39 years.

Note: The surviving four 1961-built Fairfield steam ferries referred to in *Bosphorus Ferries* were all withdrawn from service soon after the article was compiled.

Eskisehir, Kirsehir and Nevsehir

In 1955 the Turkish government-controlled company D.B. Deniz Nakliyati T.A.S. was established specially to operate cargo ships and tankers and these types of vessels were transferred to it from Denizcilik Bankasi T.A.O.

The new company's fleet included three general cargo ships of attractive appearance which had been delivered to Norwegian owners. The trio was built by Moss Vaerft & Dokk A/S, Norway and were sister ships, although each vessel had a uniquely shaped funnel.

Until the early-1970s the trio was regularly used in D.B. Deniz Nakliyati T.A.S. services between Turkish and northern European ports. Thereafter they traded for the company between Turkish and other Mediterranean or Black Sea ports only until withdrawn.

Yard no.	Completed	Name	Gross	Manager	To Turkey	Renamed
119	10/1952	*Dalheim*	2,418	Hjalmar Bjorge	1955	*Nevsehir*
120	10/1951	*Bonita*	2,413	J.M. Ugland	1953	*Kirsehir*
123	10/1953	*Bjorksund*	2,456	Hjalmar Bjorge	1953	*Eskisehir*

The *Eskisehir* (ex *Bjorksund* 1953) is seen anchored off Istanbul on 2nd May 1979. She was acquired by other Turkish interests in 1982 but sold to breakers at Aliaga and beached in July 1983. *[Nigel Jones]*

The *Kirsehir* (ex *Bonita* 1953) was photographed while idle in the Bosphorus on 5th September 1977. During the following year she was sold to Manioglu Gemi Isletmeciligi ve Tickaret A.S., Turkey and renamed *S. Manioglu*. In 1979 she was acquired by Kalkavan Denizcilik ve Tickaret A.S., Turkey and renamed *Ziya Kalkavan II*. On 1st September 1985 she arrived at Aliaga to be broken up, having been towed from Istanbul, and demolition was in progress within ten days. Notably, she was the last classic steam freighter in the Turkish merchant fleet. *[Nigel Jones]*

The *Nevsehir* (ex *Dalheim* 1955) is pictured sailing from Avonmouth on 1st September 1972. She was broken up at Aliaga, near Izmir, Turkey in 1979. *[John Wiltshire]*

Etrusk

The passenger cargo ship *Etrusk* (2,992/1938) was delivered by Netptunwerft Rostock G.m.b.H. to Turkish state-owned enterprise Denizbank Denizyollari Idaresi, which existed for only 18 months from 1st January 1938. She was then transferred to T.C. Münakalât Vekâleti Devlet Denizyollari ve Isletme and joined by her two new sisters by the same builder, *Kades* (3,085/1939) and *Tirhan* (3,088/1939). The three were of identical appearance with the exception of their funnels: the *Tirhan's* being of a more streamlined designed compared to the elegant shape of her sisters.

In 1944, as part of a restructuring programme, their owner was restyled T.C. Munakalat Vekeleti Devlet Denizyollari ve Limanlari Isletme U.M. In 1951 Denizcilik Bankasi T.A.O. (Turkish Maritime Lines) was founded essentially to conduct marine transportation services both domestically and internationally; it commenced operations in 1952 and the trio duly passed to its control. All three ships could carry up to 696 passengers and were typically engaged in round trips from Istanbul to various Turkish Black Sea ports such as Zongulak, Sinop, Samsun, Trabzon and Hopa. Other services from Istanbul included those to Sea of Marmara ports and the Mediterranean ports of Izmir, Piraeus, Tripoli and Tunis.

The trio was withdrawn from service in the mid-1970s and broken up soon afterwards. The last example was *Etrusk*, seen laid-up near Pasabahçe in the Bosphorus on 6th September 1977 minus all her lifeboats, with the exception of one on port side. Although not apparent, she was in the course of raising steam for what was believed to be her final voyage for scrapping, probably at Aliaga. Two days later much black smoke and steam was belching from her funnel, signifying her departure was imminent. *[Nigel Jones]*

Ankara (upper right)

The majestic steam turbine passenger ship *Ankara* (6,148/1927), seen anchored off Istanbul on 8th September 1977, had a very remarkable career. She had been completed a half century earlier as the *Iroquois* by Newport News Shipbuilding and Drydock Company, Virginia for the Clyde Line controlled by Atlantic, Gulf and West Indies Steamship Lines (AGWI). Typically, she operated from east coast North American ports, such as New York and Jacksonville, to Miami. In 1931 she was chartered to the Los Angeles Steamship Company after one of their vessels was wrecked. The following year another AGWI company, Mallory Line, was combined with Clyde Line to form the Clyde-Mallory Line. Notably, in 1939 *Iroquois* made one voyage for the United States Lines.

In 1940 the United States Navy purchased *Iroquois* from Clyde-Mallory Line for conversion into a hospital ship at the Atlantic Basin Iron Works, Brooklyn, New York. She was renamed *Solace* and commissioned in August 1941. She participated in several significant Second World War campaigns, carrying many thousands of patients, including Pearl Harbour in 1941, the Marianas operation in 1944 and Iwo Jima in 1945. She was awarded seven battle stars for distinguished services. The *Solace* was decommissioned in March 1946, struck from the Naval Register two months later and transferred to the Marine Commission for disposal.

In 1948 she was acquired by the Turkish Government, renamed *Ankara*, and rebuilt as a passenger ship. For much of the 1950s she was operated by Denizcilik Bankasi T.A.O., her chief roster being Istanbul to western Mediterranean ports. Between the late 1950s and 1975 she was chartered to Swan Hellenic, which concentrated on cruises to visit classical sites around the coasts and islands of Greece and Turkey. She was withdrawn from service in the late-1970s and subsequently laid up for a spell prior to delivery to breakers at Aliaga in 1981. *[Nigel Jones]*

Iskenderun

The Italian shipbuilder S.A. Ansaldo built an identical pair of handsome passenger ships, *Iskenderun* (6,570/1950) and *Samsun* (6,543/1951), which initially were operated by 'Devlet Denizyollari' until Denizcilik Bankasi T.A.O. commenced trading. These oil-fired twin-screw turbine steamers had a service speed of 16.5 knots, carried up to 644 passengers and operated principally from Istanbul to Mediterranean ports as far west as Marseilles. Intermediate ports of call included Alexandria, Beirut, Piraeus, Genoa and Naples. Another route served by the sisters was Istanbul and Izmir to Limassol and Haifa.

The *Iskenderun* is pictured near the end of her career off Istanbul on 3rd September 1977; she was subsequently laid up at the Golden Horn, Istanbul. She was eventually sold to ship breakers and arrived at Aliaga under tow from Istanbul in October 1981. The *Samsun* was also sold to Aliaga breakers and beached on 13th December 1982. *[Nigel Jones]*

239

Sozer Biraderler

In July 1946 the 3,652gt general cargo ship *Odemis* was commissioned by T.C. Münakalât Vekâleti Devlet Denizyollari ve Limanlari Isletme U.M. She had been launched by Swedish builder Oskarshamns Varv Aktiebolaget in September 1943 as the *Heimdal* for Seereederei 'Frigga' A.G., Hamburg but acquired by the Turkish company prior to completion. She was subsequently transferred to Denizcilik Bankasi T.A.O. before joining the specialist cargo ship and tanker operator D.B. Deniz Nakliyati T.A.S. in 1955. She continued in state-owned service for the next two decades. In the 1970s it was unusual for owners of small freighters with steam machinery 30 or more years old to be able to sell them for further trading. Nevertheless, in 1976 *Odemis* attracted a purchaser, Sozer Biraderler of Istanbul, and

she was renamed *Sozer Biraderler*. She was used for a while in the coal trade between Zonguldak and Istanbul but in the late-1970s was taken out of service and laid-up near Pasabahçe, where she was photographed in early May 1979. She

languished there for more than five years before finally towed to Aliaga for scrapping at the end of July 1984; work commencing within two months. *[Paul Boot]*

Istikbal

The shipyards of William Gray and Co. Ltd., West Hartlepool, which closed down in 1963, were renowned for building tramps. Between 1949 and 1960 the firm completed 20 ships of this type for Greek principals (see 'Record' 36). A dozen of these had steam machinery including the *Stratidore* (4,786/1949) which was delivered to the British-based Maritime Shipping and

Trading Co. Ltd. owned by members of the Michalinos family.

In 1962 *Stratidore* was sold to Huseyin Avni Sohotorik, Istanbul and renamed *Deniz* but in the same year became *Istikbal*. Seven years later she was acquired by Istikbal Gemisi Donatma Istiraki, Istanbul, retaining her name. Under Turkish ownership she continued tramping and, as well as Black or Mediterranean Seas ports,

visited ports in countries as diverse as Brazil, Germany, Jordan and the U.S.A.

She was photographed on 18th April 1981 near Pasabahçe, where she spent several days undergoing welding repairs to her hull. However, despite this attention, she was sold soon afterwards to Muhsin Ozer for breaking up at Aliaga and work began in early July 1981. *[Nigel Jones]*

Halis Kalkavan

In November 1925 Glasgow builder Napier and Miller delivered the 3,242gt general cargo ship *Baron Graham* to Hogarth Shipping Co. Ltd. She was fitted with a triple expansion engine by David Rowan and Co. Ltd., Glasgow, and registered at Ardrossan, the port in which her owner had its origins. In spite of the depression and slump in the late 1920s and early 1930s she, along with the rest of Hogarth's ships, managed to continue trading. In September 1939

fleet. The *Baron Graham* was one of just 19 of their vessels to survive to the close of hostilities in 1945. During the 1950s she was the subject of three changes of ownership. In 1950 she was sold to Schulte & Bruns, West Germany, and renamed *Hermann Schulte*. In April 1954 she changed hands to Riza ve Aslan Sadikoglu Ortaklari Komandit Sirketi, Turkey and was renamed *Huseyin*. Finally, in December 1958, she was acquired by Ziya Kalkavan Kollektif Sirketi, Turkey and renamed

Fast forward to 3rd September 1977, *Halis Kalkavan* is seen off Sariyer, near the Black Sea entrance to the Bosphorus. Remarkably, even after 52 years of service, she appeared much the same as when completed, with the exception of her truncated foremast. At the time she was engaged in the Zonguldak to Istanbul coal trade. She was noted, in fine fettle, still working on the same run during April 1981. However, the following year she was sold for breaking up at Aliaga and delivered

Dogan

Among the first few ships built at the Scotstoun yard of Charles Connell and Co. Ltd. after the Second World War was an identical pair of 6,722gt general cargo ships, named *Mountpark* and *Wellpark*, for Denholm Line Steamers Ltd. (managed by J. and J. Denholm Ltd). The pair was each fitted with a triple-expansion engine by David Rowan and Co. Ltd., Glasgow.

The *Mountpark*, which was completed in June 1946, was to have a relatively modest lifespan. In 1959 she was sold to Maritenia Shipping Co.

Ltd., Yugoslavia and renamed *Korcula*. In 1966 she was purchased by Paloma & Salvatori, Italy, renamed *Grifone*, but ran aground off Kalymnos Island, Aegean Sea, in December the following year and subsequently sank. In contrast, her sister was to have a career which lasted almost 50% longer.

The *Wellpark* was sold in 1958 to Shamrock Shipping Co. Ltd., founded 1897 in Larne, Northern Ireland, and renamed *Inver*. She was the largest ship ever owned by the company. In 1962 she was acquired by Nejat Dogan, Turkey and renamed *Dogan*. During

the next decade she visited ports such as Basrah in Iraq, Ashdod and Haifa in Israel and Sfax, Tunisia as well as principal Turkish ports such as Istanbul and Samsun.

Dogan is pictured off Sariyer on 3rd September 1977, 31 years to the month after being commissioned by Denholm. Within 18 months she was permanently withdrawn from service and laid up in the Golden Horn, Istanbul, to await her turn at the hands of breakers at Aliaga and work commenced on 21st April 1980. *[Nigel Jones]*

Hakan (lower left)

By the end of the 1970s tramp steamers built in the United Kingdom during the Second World War and still in existence were very few and far between. The last example of no fewer than 14 acquired by Turkish owners during the 1950s and 1960s was formerly the *Lloydcrest* (7,020/1944) completed at Port Glasgow by Lithgows Ltd. for the Junecrest Shipping Co. Ltd. She was registered at London and had a triple-expansion engine manufactured at the foundry of Rankin and Blackmore Ltd., Greenock,

which gave her a service speed of 10 knots. *Lloydcrest* was transferred to Crest Shipping Co. Ltd. in 1949 and to Nassau registry in 1956. Two years later she was sold and renamed *Sinop* on becoming a member of the Turkish state-owned fleet. In 1963 she was sold by Denizcilik Nakliyati T.A.S. to Hakan Vapuru Donatma Istiraki and renamed *Hakan*.

During the 1970s she typically traded between ports in the Black or Mediterannean Seas. Her demise was hastened by a collision with the Dutch-built, Lebanese-flag *Dragon*

(871/1955; ex *Miteria Eirini* 1977, *St. Magnus* 1977, *City of Dublin* 1967) at the Black Sea entrance to the Bosphorus. The *Dragon* sank off Anadolu Kavak and *Hakan* sustained serious damage to her bow. She was subsequently laid up off Sariyer, where she is seen at the beginning of May 1979, pending a decision by the owner as to her future. For a ship of her age, not surprisingly, repairs were considered to be uneconomical. Thus, she was sold for breaking up at Aliaga and work began in October 1979. [Paul Boot]

Manioglu

For a general cargo ship to reach a half century and still be in commercial operation is remarkable; one which continues over the age of 60, and

survived the two world wars, is truly exceptional. Nevertheless, this outstanding feat can be credited to several Turkish-owned ships, including the *Manioglu* (3,527/1913), which even

retained her original triple-expansion steam engine. She was completed as the *Arcturus* by A.G. Neptun, Rostock for D.G. Argo, Bremen but seized by the French Government at Bordeaux in 1914. In 1922 she was sold to Compagnie de Navigation Paquet, of Marseilles, but was not renamed. In 1950 she was sold to Zonguldak Vapurculuk ve Komerculuk Turk Limitet Sirketi, Istanbul and renamed *Çelikel*. In 1956 she changed ownership to Celikel Turk Ltd. Ortagligi. In 1964 she was sold to Hakan ve Manioglu Vapurlari Donatma Istiraki and renamed *Manioglu*, only her third name since being commissioned. She had a further change of ownership in 1977 to Manioglu Gemi Isletmeciligi ve Tickaret A.S. but was broken up in Turkey the following year.

Manioglu is seen at the Bosphorus coal berths on 6th September 1977 and the following day she was again photographed passing Arnavutkoy. [Nigel Jones]

H. Sefer Kalkavan

The United States Maritime Commission's vast 15-year shipbuilding programme, which commenced in 1937, included the construction at various yards of 95 small steam freighters of the N3-S type, subdivided between 36 N3-S-A1 coal burners and 59 N3-S-A2 oil burners. At the end of their military services many of the vessels were disposed of to commercial owners. In 1947 a pair of the N3-S-A2 type, each completed in 1945 by McCloskey and Company of Tampa, Florida and fitted with a six-cylinder engine by Ajax Uniflow, Corry, Pennsylvania, was acquired by T.C. Münakalât Vekâleti Devlet Denizyollari ve Limanlari Isletme U.M. The 1,865gt *John J. Jackson* was renamed *Samsun* but two years later was renamed *Hopa*, to free this name for the company's new liner under construction in Italy. The 1,870gt *Rowland T. Delano*, which had been launched as *Northern Archer*, was renamed *Ardahan*. The pair was subsequently operated by both Denizcilik Bankasi T.A.O. and, from 1955, D.B. Deniz Nakliyati T.A.S. In 1969 they were sold, each finding a private Turkish owner for further trading. Sevket Manioglu acquired *Hopa* and renamed her *Merve*; she went to breakers at Izmir in 1979. The *Ardahan* was purchased by Ziya Kalkavan Kollektif Sirketi, Istanbul and renamed *H. Sefer Kalkavan*. She also was broken up in 1979, the demolition work at Aliaga beginning in June.

H. Sefer Kalkavan is pictured, like the *Manioglu*, discharging coal at the berths located near the Europa Bridge on 6th September. *[Nigel Jones]*

Taylan Kalkavan (below left)
The *Taylan Kalkavan*, seen laid up near Pasabahçe on 18th April 1981, was the last example of a Second World War class of collier known as the *Icemaid* type. She had been completed in March 1945 as the 2,025gt *Empire Vauxhall*, one of a dozen of the type built the by Grangemouth Dockyard Co. Ltd.

The design was based on the collier *Icemaid* (1,964/1936), which had been completed by S.P. Austin and Sons, Sunderland for the Gas, Light and Coke Company, and all had names prefixed *Empire*, complying with the naming system for ships ordered by the Ministry of Shipping. In 1946 the *Empire Vauxhall* was sold to Wm. France Fenwick and Co. Ltd., London

and renamed *Braywood*. In 1959 she was sold to A. Hilmi Ozmelek ve Ogullari Donatma Istiraki, Istanbul and renamed *Abdullah*. In 1976 she was acquired by Kalkavan Denizcilik ve Ticaret A.S. and renamed *Taylan Kalkavan*. Exactly a year after the photograph was taken her demolition was in progress at Aliaga. *[Nigel Jones]*

The Turkish Government's involvement in shipping extended to many activities on the Bosphorus and beyond. To round off this selection of veteran steamers a couple of small, coal-fired steam tugs are included. The *Tekirdag 2* (above) is seen heading out of the Golden Horn,

Istanbul with her funnel lowered to pass under the Galata Bridge in May 1979. The crew seem to be enjoying their midday meal on the aft deck. She was noted still in service during October 1988.

The *Y Kapi* (below) was photographed passing Arnavutkoy

on 20th April 1981. She closely resembles the Rahmi Koc Museum's preserved *Liman 2* (50/1936) built by Kreber in Holland. However, as no details have been found about either *Tekirdag 2* or *Y Kapi* the author would welcome any information that readers may have. *[Paul Boot; Nigel Jones]*

HOLTS' CHOICE OF SPONSORS
The choice of who launched what gives a glimpse inside Liverpool shipping 1939-1980
Andrew Bell

In the spring of 1945, just 14 days after the Second World War ended in Europe, a ship for Alfred Holt's Blue Funnel Line was launched into the Tay. *Rhexenor* (10,199/1945) had been ordered by the British Ministry of War Transport as one of a class of what was known as the 'Fast Empires'. That the launch was from the Caledon yard at Dundee was no coincidence, for the controlling shareholding in the shipbuilder had been held by the Liverpool shipping company since 1917. For Blue Funnel it must have been a propitious event: in the previous five years they had lost 44 of their fleet of 88 ships owned and operated on 3rd September 1939. The task of rebuilding the fleet and reclaiming the trade on the routes along which they were to ply was vast. Every other cargo liner company in Europe was similarly challenged.

When the reluctantly-expected war broke out in 1939 the Alfred Holt partnership was completing the modernisation of their Glen Line fleet with eight ships, of which *Glenearn* (9,869/1938) was the first and the still-to-be-launched *Glenartney* (8,993/1940) the last. Alfred Holt had bought Glen Line from the liquidators of the Kylsant Crash in 1935. The purchase was strategically driven, for the company wanted Glen Line's UK East Coast loading rights within the Far East Freight Conference. With *Glenartney* coming from Caledon, it was no surprise that two similar ships were ordered as follow-ons for Blue Funnel.

The *Glengyle* (9,865/1940) was the last of this class of ships to be launched in peacetime and had been named by Miss Catherine Holt, a granddaughter of Alfred Holt (1829-1911). But when it came to floating her sister ship *Glenartney* on 27th December 1939 the honour went to Mrs Edgar Brown, the wife of Caledon's Chairman. The involvement of the wives of Caledon's management became common practice during the following six years of the war. Was this because travel between Liverpool and Dundee was difficult and considered unnecessary? Mrs Edgar Brown named *Glenartney* and sponsored *Rhexenor* in 1945. The Managing Director's wife Mrs Harvey Main named what was to have been the first of the new Blue Funnel ships, *Priam* (4) (10,029/1943), in June 1941: the ship had been ordered as long ago as 28th April 1939. The delay in completion was because the Admiralty had intended to have her completed as an Escort Aircraft Carrier which is what happened to her sister ship *Telemachus* (3): taken over on the stocks she became HMS *Activity*, commissioned in September 1942. After the war she was rebuilt in the originally intended form and named *Breconshire* (9,980/1942) - *Priam* becoming *Glenorchy*.

Of the fleet that had survived the war most ships dated back to the 1920s. The Alfred Holt partners, or

Unusually for the 'Fast Empire' design the *Rhexenor* and her sister ship *Stentor* (9,833/1946) had 118,000 cubic feet of refrigerated space and spent most of their careers in Blue Funnel's UK to Australia trade. The *Rhexenor's* accommodation was notably more spartan than her sister ship and had a different layout but both could carry 12 passengers.
[Fotoflite incorporating Skyfotos]

Photographs taken at the launch of *Glengyle* at Dundee on 18th July 1939. Within seven weeks Britain was at war and Lawrence Holt and Miss Catherine Holt were probably more apprehensive about the future of this expensive ship than they appear. At least the yard's apprentices are shown as happy: they had a busy and prosperous decade ahead in a building yard working at full stretch. *[Author's collection]*

The *Anchises* had the dubious distinction when inward bound for Shanghai in 1949 of being bombed by Chinese Nationalist aircraft in the closing stage of the civil war that resulted in the huge upheaval after Mao-Tse-tung and his communist forces took over China. A do-it-yourself salvage operation saved the two-year-old ship and she was then towed to Japan for permanent repairs. *[Fotoflite incorporating Skyfotos]*

managers as they modestly called themselves, planned one of the largest building programmes ever undertaken by a British shipping company. Excluding four Victory ships, eight Liberty ships and three ships bought off the stocks, between 1947 and 1957 thirty ships were built for the Far East trades and seven for the Australian routes. Down to the minutest detail the designs of all these new buildings were the work of the company's in-house naval architect Harry Flett (1890-1961). The largest group of the new fleet comprised the *Anchises* class of which the war-built *Telemachus* (4) (8,268/1943) was the prototype. The first of the A class was *Calchas* (7,639/1947) and it was entirely appropriate that she was launched by Mrs Evelyn Holt, wife of the company's legendary senior partner Lawrence Durning Holt (1882-1962). From Scotts, Vickers on the Tyne, Harland and Wolff and Caledon the A class came as quickly as the material from which they were built became available, in a Britain where everything was so scarce that some of the timber sheeting for the decks of the early A class ships was laid during their voyages at Hong Kong.

Having sustained their menfolk through the unrelenting challenges and tensions of a world war, it was understandable that the wives or daughters of the Alfred Holt partners should name 13 of the A class. With the prestigious (and costly) quartet of the *Peleus* class (used as the flagships of the Far East trade) and the four *Helenus* class (for the Australian trade) came famous consorts as sponsors. The wife of the Labour Government's Minister of Transport, Alfred Barnes, named the lead ship *Peleus* (10,093/1949). Always an interest close to the heart of Lawrence Holt was the company's cadet training scheme which he had founded in 1916. To the wife of Brian Heathcote, his chosen lieutenant running the Midshipmen's Department, went the fame of launching *Perseus* (10,109/1950) into the Tyne from Vickers Armstrong's yard. Another connection with the company's cadet training came when *Hector* (10,125/1950) was launched at Belfast by Mrs Clement Attlee, wife of the Prime Minister and also the mother of Midshipman Martin Attlee who was serving his apprenticeship at the time.

There is something emotional about the launch of a wanted ship that endures no matter how often witnessed by those involved in a ceremony. For the sponsor it is a climactic point of even a busy and fulfilled life. And so it was for Mrs Arnold, wife of Alfred Holt's innovative Engineering Superintendent who at the time was showing the maritime world how it was possible to run diesel engines on heavy grades of oil. On a sunny spring afternoon at Dundee she named *Diomed* (7,984/1956). Travelling with the Arnolds from Liverpool was a larger than usual group for *Diomed* was the 23rd ship of the A class and one of her roles was to replace *Calchas* as the ship manned by the company's cadets. Such was the extent of Caledon's order book that on the building berths flanking the largely intact *Diomed* was Blue Star's *Canadian Star* (6,291/1957) and, a particular object of interest, the whole double bottom of *Menelaus* (8,539/1957), the first of six ships that were the designated development of the A class. Launches into the Tay estuary were spectacular, for ships were set afloat free from drag chains and a web of moorings. Swept off on a flooding tide a new ship was captured by attendant tugs, corralled and brought back to the yard's fitting out berth. By the time *Diomed* was secured alongside the launch party and guests were at a tea party in the adapted-for-the-occasion moulding loft, speeches were made and Mrs Arnold was the holder of a wonderful experience and the owner of a large diamond brooch that filled the palm of a hand.

Down through history shipping companies have invited the consorts of commercially important persons to name ships on which their cargoes might be carried. It was no coincidence that, in 1953 when Blue Funnel opened a monthly westbound service from Far Eastern ports direct to Dublin, Mrs Bolland, wife of the Irish Ambassador in London should travel to Belfast and launch *Adrastus* (7,859/1953).

It had been a long gestation period for the eight *Priam* class before they were delivered in 1966-1968: they modernised - particularly in cargo handling - the Far East

As often happened in Blue Funnel's history the ship that bore the name of the class, *Anchises*, was not the first to be launched. On a fine rain-free 27th August 1946 in Belfast, Evelyn Holt is about to send the *Calchas* down the ways to be completed as Blue Funnel's first ship to be manned by their trainee officers. At the time Lawrence Holt was trying to get British ship owners to jointly build a full-scale sailing ship for training purposes - he never succeeded. [Author's collection]

One P class sailed from Birkenhead for Rotterdam and the Far East on the 13th of every month. With a service speed of 18 knots, consuming 72 tonnes of fuel oil a day, they were for many years amongst the fastest ships on the route. Although built to call at Chinese mainland ports they never did so and, for this reason, their 70,360 cubic feet of reefer space was seldom used although their seven cargo oil tanks were. The P's passenger accommodation was exactly the same as that of the *Helenus* class. Whilst waiting for her sister ships to be completed the *Peleus* made her maiden voyage to Australia - a useful exercise to show the shippers what the H class would be like. [Fotoflite incorporating Skyfotos]

All the *Anchises* class had accommodation for 12 passengers on the port side of the promenade decks. The passengers' lounge was amidships and one deck below was an airy dining saloon shared with all the officers. Merseysiders, never slow to nickname a ship, knew successive ships named *Adrastus* as 'A.D.Rastus'. [Airfoto of Malacca/J. and M. Clarkson]

express services. Four were designated for Blue Funnel's use and four for Glen Line. Lady Chambers, wife of Sir Paul, Chairman of ICI, named *Peisander* (12,094/1967), and *Glenfinlas* (12,094/1967) was sponsored by Mrs E.K. Swire of the dominant Swire Group. Two of the class were the first ships Alfred Holt had built in Japan. No doubt through the Swire connections, Princess Chichibu, sister-in-law of Emperor Hirohito, named *Glenalmond* (13,575/1966) and a Mrs Asaki, wife of a man who must have been a very senior Japanese civil servant in their Foreign Office, did the honours for *Pembrokeshire* (12,299/1967). It was a different story for the ships of the class being built on Tyneside. So bad had relations become between owners and Vickers the builders - mainly over late deliveries by as much as one year - that there were no official sponsors for *Protesilaus* (12,094/1967) and *Radnorshire* (12,089/1967). However, Marshall Meek, Ocean's well known naval architect who was in charge of the five ships being built on the Tyne, was not going to let the last two ships be launched unchristened, so two of his staff assigned to the yard, Bob Kay and Jimmy White, duly named them before they entered the Tyne: there was no formal ceremony. The reaction, if any, back in India Buildings head office in Liverpool, is unrecorded.

An essential part of any cargo liner company's service are their port agents. With Blue Funnel's and Glen Line's spread

On the building berth behind the *Glenfinlas* is the hull of yard number 736, the yet to be named at her launch nine months later, *Queen Elizabeth 2*. There was a folk tale amongst the staff of Blue Funnel that much of the cost of the *Glenfinlas* was offset by the penalty claims on the *Centaur* delivered late, three years previously. *[John Brown and Co. (Clydebank) Ltd./J. and M. Clarkson collection]*

across the world it was natural that agents from ports such as New York should provide sponsors, as they did for *Cyclops* (7,709/1948). Those from Singapore were involved with *Autolycus* (7,705/1949) and *Glenfalloch* (11,918/1963); from Amsterdam with *Laertes* (7,664/1949); from Djkarta with *Laomedon* (7,864/1953); from Glasgow with *Lycaon* (7,859/1954); from Japanese ports with *Atreus* (7,800/1951) and *Antenor* (7,974/1956). The Australian ports' agents scored particularly well by

Glenfalloch was one of the four *Glenlyons,* the last ships to be designed by Harry Flett who did not live to see them in service. Many considered them to be the finest ships that Alfred Holt ever built. They could carry 10,000 tonnes at 21 knots with their 18,250 horsepower Sulzer engines consuming 69 tonnes per day. Their 82,680 cubic feet of reefer space was largely used for carrying Chinese-produced meat and eggs to the Eastern European countries of the Soviet Empire, via Hamburg. As containerisation was introduced into the Far Eastern trades a detailed study was undertaken to convert the *Glenlyons* to be used as container ships for Elder Dempster's primary trades in place of the passenger-cargo mailboats: it never happened. *[Fotoflite incorporating Skyfotos]*

The *Jason* was the only ship Blue Funnel ever had built by Swan Hunter who took the opportunity to flamboyantly decorate the public rooms and spaces with fancy metal work and engraved glass. Considered to be the prestige ships for the Australian trade, they originally carried 23 passenger in lower berths and an extra six in upper Pullmans making the total 29. Their cargo deadweight was over 11,000 tonnes carried in 500,000 cubic feet of space for general cargo in addition to which there was 125,120 cubic feet of refrigerated space at the forward end of the long centre-castle. The smears on the ship's side were caused by waste water discharges: the Holt tradition was that you had as few apertures under the water line as you could manage. *[Airfoto of Malacca/J. and M. Clarkson]*

being involved in ships' early lives with Perth's agent's wife sponsoring *Nestor* (4) (7,802/1952) and Brisbane's *Neleus* (7,802/1953). Lady Goss, wife of the long-serving Chairman of Adelaide Steamship who was also the head of George Wills and Co., the Adelaide and Perth agents, named *Jason* (10,160/1950), the only ship that Swan Hunter ever built for Blue Funnel. When the unusual passenger cargo ship *Centaur* (8,262/1964) went down the ways from John Brown's yard in 1963 it was Mrs David Brand, wife of the Western Australian Premier, who named her.

There was an unusual coincidence that involved three of the four *Glenlyons*, all launched in 1962. At the time

Lady MacTier and Peter Goedkoop, Managing Director of the builders Nederlandsche Dok & Scheepsbouw Maatschappij, at the launch of *Glenlyon* at Amsterdam on 17th March 1962.

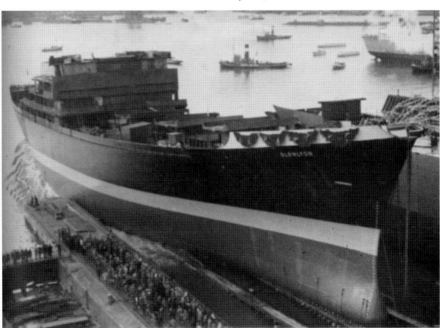

Lady MacTier was the wife of Sir Stewart, a Glen Line, London man who was promoted to the partnership in Liverpool after the sudden death of W.H. Dickie. As Blue Funnel's Technical Director he and Marshall Meek were much involved in the design and building of Overseas Container Lines' pioneering *Discovery Bay* class of five ships. *[Author's collection]*

Built to Silver Lines' specifications, the *Ulysses* was delivered with a wide range of equipment that was not standard and often superior to that of all the other units of the Blue Funnel fleet. Stories were legion about what was taken off the ship after delivery. One feature that did survive was 'The Inn' on the boat deck, fitted out as an Olde English Pub years before the officers' lounges had bars. The Simplex steel cargo hatch covers were another first time feature.
[B. and A. Feilden/J. and M. Clarkson]

individual sons of the three sponsors Mesdames Keswick of Jardines, Smith of Glen Line and Roper-Coldbeck of the Singapore agents were all working in Singapore far removed from the launching ceremonies which took place in May, June and July. Perhaps the oddest of all involved three of the four of a class of Silver Line ships bought by Alfred Holt when they were still under construction by J.L. Thompson at Sunderland. At the time the builders had a substantial stake in the shipping line that they had helped create in 1925. All three ships were launched into the Wear in 1949-1950 by three Silver Line sponsors who briefly gave them names prefixed *Silver* which they never carried. Was it for taxation reasons? The ships were *Silverholly* which became *Ulysses* (8,976/1949), *Silverelm* which became *Teiresias* (8,924/1950) and *Silverlaurel* (8,922/1950) which became *Teucer*.

The only ship launched without a sponsor was *Menelaus*: this was on 15th March 1957. She was to have been named on 14th February but labour problems at Caledon delayed the launch. There is no record surviving as to whom the sponsor was to be. The five sisters of *Menelaus*

Antilochus was one of six Mark II *Anchises* class fitted out to carry over 1,000 unberthed Moslem pilgrims, hence the extra life boats over the seaman's house and on the poop: the six sets of davits amidships could also have a double stack of lifeboats. Port holes can be seen in the hull behind which cargo was normally carried. In addition to the centre-castle, the well decks were timber sheathed and when carrying pilgrims all six cargo hatches had canvas awnings over them - the ship looked like a floating circus tent.
[B. and A. Feilden/J. and M. Clarkson]

Owned by the Ocean group - as Blue Funnel became - for only four years, the *Titan* was a one-off ship built in Sweden. In the early 1970s Ocean had a scatter-gun approach to diversification which irreverently became known as 'where shall we lose £1million this year?' amongst the staff ashore and afloat. *[Fotoflite incorporating Skyfotos]*

were luckier. The managing partners must have all been absent from India Buildings, Liverpool on 2nd November 1948 when Lady Rebbeck named *Antilochus* (7,635/1949) in her husband's yard at Belfast and Mrs Nelson, wife of the company's Nautical Adviser, launched *Automedon* (8,236/1949) at Newcastle.

Did the almost puritanical Unitarian lives of the senior management preclude invitations to members of the Royal Family so usual amongst the other large British shipping companies? National celebrities were never considered despite the Beatles' Cavern Club being within a minute's walk of India Buildings. A neat coincidence occurred at Dundee on 10th April 1948 when Mrs Prowie, wife of the city's Lord Provost,

named *Clytoneus* (7,680/1949) for his Lordship's employment was as a Caledon shipyard worker. He was able to say in a speech afterwards that he had been responsible for the ship's stern frame.

The most frequent sponsor of all was Lady Maud Alexander, wife of the Chairman, as Blue Funnel, Glen Line and Elder Dempster became the Ocean Group, for she named the VLCC *Titan* (113,551/1971), the LNG tanker *Nestor* (5) (78,915/1977) and the second M class *Mentor* (16,482/1980) - all three within eight years.

Who launched what gives a glimpse of colour and personality to a shipping empire's proud story so often untold when a fleets' details are remembered and recorded.

SOURCES AND ACKNOWLEDGEMENTS

We thank all who gave permission for their photographs to be used, and for help in finding photographs we are particularly grateful to Tony Smith, Jim McFaul and David Whiteside of the World Ship Photo Library; to Ian Farquhar, F.W. Hawks, Peter Newall, William Schell, George Scott; and to David Hodge and Bob Todd of the National Maritime Museum, and other museums and institutions listed.

Research sources have included the *Registers* of William Schell and Tony Starke, 'Lloyd's Register', 'Lloyd's Confidential Index', 'Lloyd's Shipping Index', 'Lloyd's War Losses', 'Mercantile Navy Lists', 'Marine News', 'Sea Breezes' and 'Shipbuilding and Shipping Record'. Use of the facilities of the World Ship Society, the Guildhall Library, the National Archives and Lloyd's Register of Shipping and the help of Dr Malcolm Cooper are gratefully acknowledged. Particular thanks also to Heather Fenton for editorial and indexing work, and to Marion Clarkson for accountancy services.

Turkish veteran steamers
Many thanks to Paul Boot for his considerable help and very valuable input both with the research process and, of course, the photographs. Thanks also to Bill Schell, Graham Thursby and Malcolm Cranfield. In addition to sources noted above, information came from: W.H. Mitchell and L.A. Sawyer 'The Empire Ships' (Lloyd's of London Press, 1990); L.A. Sawyer and W.H. Mitchell 'From America to United States' Part Four (World Ship Society; 1986); N.L. Middlemiss 'Travels of the Tramps' Volume IV (Shields Publications, 1993); I.G. Stewart 'British Tramps' (Ian Stewart Marine Publications, 1997); A.A. McAlister and Leonard Gray 'H. Hogarth and Sons Limited' (World Ship Society, 1976).

The last voyage of *Hemsley-I*
Thanks to RFA expert Tom Adams for checking the text and help with images.

LIBERTY SHIPS ON CHARTER TO BRITAIN
Part 3: minor incidents
John de S. Winser

Part 1 provided the background to the Liberty ships chartered to Britain by the United States, and Part 2 detailed the major damage and losses incurred by this 182-strong fleet. To extend the picture of events and the problems involving these ships and their crews, Part 3 records some of the many lesser incidents which took place during the five-year period between July 1943, when *Samholt* became the first vessel delivered to Britain, and 1948 when the last operational vessels were handed back to the United States Maritime Commission.

Lost propellers
In service, Liberty ships encountered tail shaft faults and no fewer than nine 'Sam' ships lost their single screws in 1946-47. The first was *Sambanka* while sailing from Rangoon to Lourenco Marques (Mozambique), following which Lyle Shipping's *Cape Wrath* towed her into Diego Suarez (Madagascar) on 25th February 1946. With no spare tail shaft or propeller on board, *Sambanka* left for Durban on 26th March in the tow of the Sunderland-registered *Empire Kinsman* but an uncontrollable fire in that ship's bunkers forced her to deviate to Beira (Mozambique). Arriving there on 1st April, the plan was for the Canadian-owned *Fort St Antoine* to take over the tow but the prospect of bad weather resulted in the British Tanker Company's *British Sincerity*, which was standing by, being employed for the task. By coincidence, the next five ships disabled by propeller loss were all destined for Vancouver. *Samarkand* left Shanghai on 19th July 1946 and another Alfred Holt ship, *Ajax*, came

to her aid, on 3rd August towing her into Yokohama, at which port, for the same reason, *Samadre* arrived on 6th September, after a three-day tow by HM cruiser *Euryalus*. Having transitted the Panama Canal on passage from London, *Samnebra* was stranded 265 miles from Balboa and had to return there on 9th August in the tow of the Canadian *Rondeau Park*. Also in the Pacific, *Samleyte* lost her propeller and the use of her rudder south of San Diego (California) whilst sailing from Glasgow: the US Coast Guard cutter *Perseus* and tug *Kanak* came to her rescue, the tug and her tow moving at 5.61 knots to complete the 525-mile voyage to Los Angeles on 23rd September. On 6th November *Samjack* reported that she had been similarly disabled on passage from Singapore and a naval tug was allocated for the two-week tow to Pearl Harbor. This also became the arrival port for *Samidway* towed by a naval tug on 30th January 1947, after losing her propeller 270 miles west of Honolulu on passage from Shanghai. Meanwhile, in the Mediterranean, whilst sailing from Port Said to West Africa, *Sambrian* had become propeller-less in position 31.43 north by 31.48 east and reached Alexandria on 5th September 1946 towed by *Saminver*. Bound from Durban to Montevideo, *Samwinged* shed her screw 1,000 miles west of Capetown: because it was out of range of local tugs, the London-registered *Fort Frobisher* came to her assistance, towing her into Table Bay on 30th April 1947. The final ship was *Samtruth*, 800 miles off Bermuda, bound from Avonmouth to Mobile (Alabama) that 20th December: she reached Bermuda on the second day of 1948, in the tow of

Conspicuous in this photograph of *Sambrian,* taken at Wellington, New Zealand are the tall booms which, when fitted with nets and lowered beside the ship, provided anti-torpedo protection. *[Ian J. Farquhar]*

Heavy weather encountered by *Samarovsk* during her maiden voyage across the Pacific caused damage to her steering gear, fittings and cargo. *[Photo GVM/Copyright Flor van Otterdyk]*

the Manchester-registered *Fort McLoughlin*, after which she was handed over to the American tug *Eugene F Moran* for the final sector to Charleston (South Carolina).

9th September 1943: *Samovar*
Bound from San Francisco on the Pacific route to Egypt, the ship located the disabled Anglo-Saxon tanker *Trocas*, drifting more than 1,200 miles from New Zealand, without power and with her rudder jammed hard to port. After battling with two broken tows and a severe three-day gale, the 18-day ordeal ended safely when the two ships reached Auckland on 27th September.

11th-20th September 1943: *Samson*
Sailing westwards towards the Indian Ocean from Hobart, gale-force conditions resulted in *Samson's* forward port lifeboat being washed overboard and a landing barge and tank, stowed on number 2 hatch, twice breaking away.

1st October 1943: *Samarovsk*
Heavy weather in the Pacific necessitated the ship putting into Wellington for a stay of 17 days during her voyage from Los Angeles to Ceylon and India: repairs were carried out to steering gear and deck fittings, storm-damaged items from number 3 'tween deck were discharged for reconditioning and collapsed deck cargo on number 5 hatch was re-stowed.

10th February 1944: *Samota*
During the trans Atlantic sector of her voyage from New York to Naples, a sick donkeyman was transferred by breeches buoy for treatment aboard the escorting USS *Douglas L. Howard*. The patient died soon after embarking in the destroyer and his body was returned to *Samota* for burial at sea that evening.

15th February 1944: *Samforth*
During a crossing from New York to the Central

Mediterranean in convoy (UGS 32) the US *Haym Salomon*, sailing at 10 knots on a parallel course to *Samforth*, suddenly swung out of line at 01.05. Her stem penetrated over 16 feet into *Samforth's* starboard hull, creating a hole 15 feet wide from her main deck to below the water-line, just forward of the bridge. While extricating herself, she grazed *Samforth's* lifeboats, davits and bulwarks. Despite this damage and with water to a depth of 25 feet in number 3 hold, the convoy was rejoined until reaching Oran (Algeria) on 20th February. Damage included shell plates, frames, bulkheads, lower and upper navigation bridges, bulwarks and two lifeboats. On the ship's return passage from Bone (Algeria) to Baltimore, flooding in number 3, the hold badly damaged during her outward voyage, forced the vessel to put into Bermuda on 20th April.

19th February 1944: *Samgara*
At Bermuda, the First Mate lost his life in attempting to grapple for a chain which had lodged around the ship's rudder during a westbound transAtlantic crossing to New York. He was leaning over the side of a lifeboat which unexpectedly swung beneath the ship's counter, causing his head to be crushed.

12th March 1944: *Samlong*
Two days after leaving Calcutta for the UK an urgent message was transmitted to the escorting warship to remove a donkeyman, who had grabbed the Chief Officer by the throat and threatened the Master. Next day, the man left the ship under escort provided by an incoming naval vessel.

1st April 1944: *Samcalia* and *Samuta*
Samcalia, sailing between Aden and Karachi, rescued some of the survivors from the US *Richard Hovey*, torpedoed by a Japanese submarine three days earlier. Another lifeboat with 38 crew members aboard remained at sea for another two weeks until discovered by *Samuta*.

A number of crew members of a torpedoed US Liberty ship owed their April 1944 rescue to the timely arrival on the scene of *Samcalia,* seen in Auckland, New Zealand. *[Ships in Focus collection]*

18th April 1944: *Samtroy*
The Master was informed, after the vessel's arrival in New York from the Mediterranean, that 21 crew members had lodged a petition at the British Consulate requesting his removal for arrogant, domineering and provocative behaviour. An inquiry was held and the Master was absolved.

4th May 1944: *Samsoaring*
An explosion on board the vessel at her builder's fitting out dock at Baltimore caused the ship to list towards the quay and rapidly fill with water. Engineers managed to get her onto an even keel and she settled on the bottom in 20 feet of water. After emergency repairs she was raised, floated to the repair berth and by 29th May was in a fit state for delivery.

Samsoaring is seen here listing heavily to port following an explosion while the ship was fitting out at Baltimore. *[J. and M. Clarkson collection]*

7th May 1944: *Samfoyle*
On leaving Boston for the Tyne the vessel's cargo included 533 tons on deck, comprising 5-ton carriers and 27-ton tanks, with four carriers and two tanks stowed on number 1 hatch; two of each on number 3 and the remaining 15 carriers and 12 tanks distributed equally across numbers 2, 4 and 5 hatches.

25th May 1944: *Samida*
Sailing from Bombay in ballast, the ship grounded six miles from Karachi. During refloating operations with the aid of the tug *Rose* on 31st May her starboard anchor and 90 fathoms of cable had to be slipped; her windlass piston became bent and eight feet of her port side bilge keel was wrenched off and twisted.

27th May 1944: *Sambre*
Off Taranto, *Sambre*'s propeller became fouled when a wire fell overside during preparations for cargo work. The Italian corvette *Cormorano* towed the ship into port and, a week later, she was tipped and her propeller cleared.

8th June 1944: *Samos* and *Sammont*
Two days after D-Day, the Chief Engineer and an engine room crew member of *Samos* and the Chief Officer and three others aboard *Sammont* suffered injuries from shell splinters at Juno beachhead, Normandy.

8th July 1945: *Samsperrin*
A day after leaving Baltimore for Birkenhead, the vessel grounded at full speed in position 37.52 north by 75.13 west at 14.19. Initial refloating attempts failed, even after pumping out 800 tons of oil fuel and 120 tons of water and receiving assistance from local naval and coastguard vessels. *Samsperrin* was finally released at 01.00 on 11th July, with the aid of a US salvage tug, and put into New York the following day.

Photographed on the Scheldt, *Samos* was one of 22 British Liberty ships which had served Normandy after the D-Day landings in 1944. Two of her crew were injured by enemy fire on 8th June. *[Photo GVM/Copyright Flor van Otterdyk]*

13th July 1944: *Samnebra*
Because the vessel was undermanned, seamen refused to move the ship at Bone (Algeria) without extra pay. She was therefore warped along the quay by the Bosun, Carpenter and gunners and her sailing delayed by three days.

22nd July 1944: *Samshee*
Distress rockets observed from the bridge, whilst the ship was proceeding between Colombo and Aden, resulted in 23 survivors on rafts being rescued from Dodd, Thomson's *King Frederick*, sunk by a U-boat three days earlier.

4th August 1944: *Samselbu*
During her stay at Normandy's Gold beachhead, discharging a cargo of stores from Birkenhead, part of a German aircraft

crashed on the vessel's fore deck during a night-time attack on the assembled fleet.

13th August 1944: *Samwash*
One of 14 'Sam' ships supporting the landings in the South of France, *Samwash* left Naples with 52 ground vehicles, 28 amphibious vehicles, two landing craft and 243 troops. After her arrival at Camel beachhead two days later, three crew members suffered wounds from shrapnel from ships' anti-aircraft fire.

7th August 1944: *Samvern*
While awaiting the departure of her convoy from the Thames to Normandy, a fire was extinguished in two of the vehicles stowed in number 5 hold. At sea, four days

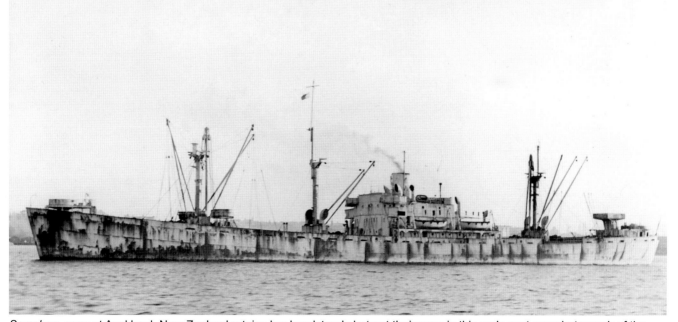

Samshee, seen at Auckland, New Zealand retains her bandstands but not their guns in this early post-war photograph of the ship showing signs of prolonged sea service. *[Ian J. Farquhar]*

later, the Chief Engineer reported the urgent need to stop the engines for repairs to a badly leaking injection pipe. As *Samvern* was by then in the mineswept approaches to Juno beach in a strong cross tide, there was little alternative but to sail on for a further four hours and for the start of repairs to await arrival at her beachhead anchorage.

6th September 1944: *Samvigna*
On passage from Colombo, a crashed RAF Wellington bomber was sighted north of Socotra Island at 04.30 but no aircrew could be seen. Eight hours later, a dinghy containing three men was spotted, with another man 200-300 yards away. All four survivors were brought aboard and taken to Aden.

11th September 1944: *Samois*
On its way to the anchorage at Marseilles, a local boat carrying stevedores to work cargo on *Samois* suddenly capsized as it approached the ship, drowning seven of its 60 occupants.

15th September 1944: *Samavon*
The Chief Engineer, returning to his ship at Port de Bouc (South of France) by US Army lorry, required hospitalisation after sustaining injuries as a result of the vehicle being attacked by six roadside bandits.

17th September 1944: *Sampa*
On entering London's Tilbury Dock at the end of her fifth round voyage to the Normandy beaches, the vessel rammed and sank the drifter HMS *Mirabelle*, which was lying alongside Berth 26.

27th September 1944: *Sammont*
A head-on collision with the jetty dented and buckled the ship's plating on arrival at London's King George V Dock from Normandy. Although 'full astern' had been ordered, the engines had inadvertently been put to 'full ahead.'

20th October 1944: *Samhorn*
In convoy from Halifax to London, violent rolling in a heavy Atlantic swell caused her accommodation to become flooded; her forward port raft and after port lifeboat to be swept overboard and the forward port lifeboat to be forced inboard with such velocity that both davits were rendered useless.

27th November 1944: *Samana*
The ship left Piraeus for Port Said carrying German prisoners-of-war.

28th November 1944: *Samhope* and *Samlea*
Completing their voyages to Antwerp from New York, *Samhope* and *Samlea* were two of 12 ships comprising the first ocean-going cargo ship convoy to be directed to the Belgian port since its liberation.

29th December 1944: *Sameveron*
In convoy (ON 273) from London to New York, the ship encountered hurricane-force winds in position 44.35 north by 47.02 west at 04.30. A 50-degree list to starboard developed, all the stone and sand ballast shifted, number 1 lifeboat and raft were carried away, number 2 lifeboat was blown inboard and its bottom damaged, number 3 lifeboat was stove in and the ship's engines stopped because of exposure above water-level of the main injection valve. All available crew were urgently put to work shifting ballast from the starboard side of the 'tween decks to the port side of the lower holds and this, together with improving weather conditions, resulted in the list gradually being reduced. By the afternoon of 31st December, steaming could be resumed with St John's (Newfoundland) being reached on 2nd January. After a five day stay, during which a new lifeboat and raft were supplied and the engines and damaged lifeboats repaired, the ship resumed her voyage. Had details of this incident been circulated to all shipowners and managers, the post-war loss of *Samkey*, in similar circumstances, might have been avoided. (See the 31st January 1948 entry in Part 2 of this article.)

The forward port raft is missing in this post-war photograph of *Samhorn* taken at Dunedin on 16th May 1946. A raft in this position was swept overboard during an October 1944 Atlantic crossing. *[Ian J. Farquhar]*

Five months after a grounding incident at Falmouth in December 1944, *Samythian* embarked on a nine-week voyage to North Russian ports. *[Ships in Focus collection]*

31st December 1944: *Samythian*
Attempting to leave Falmouth, after calling there whilst on passage from New York to Antwerp, the vessel found HM Trawler *Bombardier* to be blocking the channel. To avoid a collision, *Samythian* was run onto a mud bank, where she remained stuck for nearly six hours.

1st January 1945: *Samchess*
After leaving the Clyde for New York on 24th December, the ship joined her convoy (ON 274) and, eight days out, faced a north-easterly gale. Very heavy rolling in a high, confused sea caused the 'tween deck slag ballast to shift and an alarming list to port resulted, to such an extent that the port after raft disappeared overboard. The vessel hove to while all available hands were mustered to work in the holds. The following day the list was reduced to 15 degrees but it was three days before it was down to 5 degrees, by which time the weather had moderated sufficiently for the vessel to work up to full speed and rejoin the convoy. This incident occurred three days after *Sameveron* experienced a similar situation (see above).

4th January 1945: *Samarina*
Carrying a cargo of 179 military vehicles from London to Antwerp, the vessel was in position 51.21 north by 3.01 east near Zeebrugge at 11.10, when a suspicious craft, later identified as a midget submarine, was sighted at a range of 400-500 yards. One of *Samarina*'s twin and two of her single Oerlikon guns opened fire and a sinking was confirmed by the escorting destroyer HMS *Mendip*.

8th January 1945: *Samtyne*
During a storm the vessel broke from her pier moorings at Halifax, collided with a barge and with the Glasgow-registered *Tenax* and went ashore in the harbour. With damage to three starboard plates and two propeller blades, the ship refloated and entered drydock for repairs.

8th January 1945: *Saminver*
A day after the vessel reached Antwerp from London, a German V2 rocket exploded in the river in close proximity to her starboard side. Blast damage injured two crew members, affected the ship's upper works, bridge and accommodation and caused the slight setting in of her starboard side. After being drydocked for repairs at Antwerp, she left again 19 days later.

19th January 1945: *Samsoaring*
The day before reaching Hull from St John's (Newfoundland), the ship was pitching so heavily in a very steep sea that buckling occurred across the deck and down the hull on both sides at number 4 hold and, to a lesser degree, also at number 5. It was more than seven weeks before remedial work enabled her to start her next voyage from Hull to Newcastle and Montreal.

22nd January 1945: *Samfield*
When smoke started emanating from number 1 hatch two days after leaving Port Said, steam extinguishers were employed and the vessel diverted to Tobruk (Libya). With the fire still not fully extinguished, on 25th January the vessel returned to Alexandria, where the hold was flooded, then pumped out, revealing, after discharge of cargo, the buckling of 'tween deck beams and deck plating, despite which, within 16 days, she was ready to sail for Naples.

24th January 1945: *Samtrent*
After discharging cargo from New York at Antwerp, the ship had left for the Tyne the previous day and was turning at slow speed to anchor off the Kent coast in patchy fog, when a collision with the London-registered coaster *Crane* ripped a 10 by 5 foot hole in her port bow at number 1 'tween deck.

24th-29th January 1945: *Samdonard*
Heavy weather between Halifax and Liverpool resulted in

The day after arriving at Antwerp in January 1945, *Saminver* took the blast of a German V2 rocket which exploded in close proximity to her. *[Imperial War Museum A23033]*

one lifeboat, together with its davits, being swept overboard and the other three lifeboats being stove in and filled with water. This, combined with damage to deck fittings and to number 1 hold, caused the vessel to leave the convoy to hove to and consequently reach Liverpool one day late.

20th February 1945: *Samchess*
A double collision occurred whilst the ship was completing a voyage from New York. Firstly, her port bow was cut to the water-line when the London-registered *Northleigh* crossed in front, then, whilst proceeding back to Margate Roads anchorage, she lost both port lifeboats and had the shell plating at number 3 hold punctured by being hit by the US-flag *William Floyd*. Making water fast, with her damaged hold flooded to sea level, *Samchess* reached London (Tilbury) at reduced speed on 27th February, before later continuing to Antwerp.

20th February 1945: *Samark*
The port side of number 1 hold was the impact area in a collision with the Hain-managed *Empire General*, when *Samark* was arriving at Antwerp from London. After repairs, she sailed on 22nd February, only to be badly holed, above and below the water-line on the port side amidships, in a collision with the US-flag *Jonathan Elmer*. *Samark* was beached for temporary repairs by *American Salvor*, refloated with the aid of the tug *Antic*, then put back to Antwerp for further repairs.

27th February 1945: *Samglory*
On reaching Naples anchorage from Marseilles, the port anchor, lowered in readiness for dropping, fouled an obstruction on the bottom, ran out 135 fathoms of cable and damaged the windlass.

5th March 1945: *Samteviot*
Number 1 port derrick became strained as a result of its improper use to haul rail trucks along the adjoining quayside at Baltimore, while the ship was loading cargo for Karachi and Bombay.

21st March 1945: *Samholt*
Heading from Rosario and Buenos Aires to Belfast, the ship put into Pernambuco (Brazil) steaming only on her starboard boiler, because 30 new tubes were needed for her port boiler. *Samthar*, sailing from Buenos Aires one week after *Samholt*, called at Pernambuco to supply 16 tubes, while the others were forwarded from Rio de Janeiro.

9th April 1945: *Samspeed*
A massive explosion of ammunition being discharged at Bari (Italy) from the US *Charles Henderson* partially sank her and affected all vessels in the immediate vicinity, including *Samspeed*, in which her Master, Third Mate, Bosun and 16 crew members suffered injury. Heavy wreckage was thrown onto her decks, her accommodation sustained fire damage and her upper deck plating became distorted. Temporarily repaired but certificated only for the carriage of light cargo, the ship was able to leave on 13th May for permanent repairs at Antwerp.

11th April 1945: *Sampford*
On passage from New York to London in heavy Atlantic seas, at 03.00 the vessel's forward port lifeboat sustained damage; violent rolling at 04.15 resulted in her forward starboard life raft being lost overboard and, at 17.30, the starboard after lifeboat was carried away.

12th April 1945: *Samhope*
Although all shore leave had been stopped, no fewer than 23 crew members were missing at sailing time from Glasgow. Almost all subsequently returned to the ship but by that time she had missed her transAtlantic convoy to Montreal.

14th April 1945: *Samport*
On arriving at Antwerp from Southampton, the vessel took a sheer to port in a strong ebb tide and, as a result, struck and seriously damaged HMS *Lune*, as well as crushing the trawler's launch.

Strick Line's *Serbistan* served as *Samglory* from 1944 until her change of name in 1947. *[Photo GVM/Copyright Flor van Otterdyk]*

17th April 1945: *Samtredy*
The ship arrived at Leghorn (Italy) where naval orders stipulated that, for security reasons, all vessels must run their main engines slow astern between 19.00 and 07.00, that all hands should be kept on sea watches and that bottom lines should be worked along the keel and bilge keels every four hours to detect any obstruction.

22nd May 1945: *Samglory*
A hurricane hit Montreal when the vessel was alongside the bulk wheat loading berth at 16.00. The forward moorings carried away and, caught by both wind and current, the ship pivoted on her stern lines which still held. Letting go both anchors failed to prevent the vessel causing considerable damage to the wooden auxiliary schooner *St Simeon C.* Attempts were started at 17.40 to re-berth *Samglory* using the ship's engines and two tugs but the strength of the wind and lashing rain meant that it was 22.30 before this manoeuvre was finally accomplished.

22nd May 1945: *Samneagh*
A crew member re-boarded at Santiago de Cuba, claiming he had been threatened on the quayside by someone with a revolver. In retaliation, he trained one of the ship's Oerlikon guns onto the shore but, in his intoxicated state, was unable to fire it.

27th May 1945: *Samaustral*
In position 43.19 north by 28.57 west, when leading column 4 of her westbound transAtlantic convoy (ON 303) in dense fog, *Samaustral* struck an iceberg with her starboard bow. The impact twisted her stem; caused damage above the water-line for 20 feet aft and 10 to 15 feet upwards and crushed her starboard anchor inboard, rendering it useless. Temporary repairs were effected using mattresses and cement. St. John (New Brunswick) was reached before the ship moved to Halifax for permanent repairs. As work was being completed on 18th July, the ship started ranging heavily alongside because of violent explosions, after a serious fire broke out in the Royal Canadian Navy magazine. *Samaustral* was moved out and well clear of the harbour until the fire had been contained and it was deemed safe for her to return.

31st May 1945: *Samgara*
When steering a ship's lifeboat at Bombay, the Third Officer fell overboard, presumably after losing his balance, and was never seen again.

6th July 1945: *Samteviot*
At the intended sailing time from Buenos Aires, so many crew members had returned drunk and incapable that departure for South Africa was postponed by one day for safety reasons.

23rd July 1945: *Samderwent*
Carrying coal from Philadelphia to Stavanger (Norway), the vessel was in collision off the Kent coast with the anchored US *Cornelius Harnett*, as a result of a strong flood tide and the slowness of the ship to answer the helm. Holed from the water-line to the upper deck on the starboard side of number 2 hatch, *Samderwent* was diverted to the Thames, where, two days later, she was further delayed by going aground outside Tilbury Dock.

26th July 1945: *Samglory*
On the eve of leaving New York for India, the ship's engineers carried out repairs to the steering gear, after what was strongly suspected to have been an act of sabotage.

10th August 1945: *Samteviot*
The vessel arrived at Port Louis (Mauritius) with a deck cargo from Durban consisting of Admiralty fishing vessels and small boats, one of which, during discharge, was damaged by being dropped into the hatch.

18th August 1945: *Samcree*
The vessel left Lome (Togoland) for a passage to Casablanca through such boisterous seas that water damage affected her cargo of coffee, cocoa, palm-kernels, palm oil and tapioca.

20th August 1945: *Samarkand*
When the ship was at Geelong (Australia), the Chief Officer and four seamen died of asphyxiation in number 2 starboard deep tank and five crew members were taken to hospital suffering from the effects of fumes.

28th August 1945: *Samgara* and *Samgaudie*
These two vessels formed part of a fleet of cargo ships carrying troops, vehicles, equipment and stores to the 9th September Malayan landings. One day out from Bombay the hull of *Malika*, one of the other ships in the assault convoy (JMA1S), sustained a 5½-inch hull puncture below the water-line, and subsequent flooding, from a shell fired from a Bofors gun stowed in her hold. When the guns in all the ships had arrived at the quay, the order that they should be 'loaded' had been totally misinterpreted. As soon as events aboard *Malika* revealed the mistake, the ammunition in all the ships was immediately removed at sea. On 8th September the Officer Commanding Troops aboard *Samgaudie* fell into her lower hold between the vehicles. The following day, still unconscious, he was transferred in HM frigate *Loch Quoich* to the Dutch hospital ship *Ophir* but later died.

8th September 1945: *Samdon*
A serious fire in the engine room, whilst the vessel was refuelling from a lighter at New York, took more than four hours to contain: the blaze was caused by the starboard boiler overheating then collapsing, owing to a lack of water. With the cost of repairs estimated at $50,000, the vessel was, on 5th October, secured off Staten Island, New York, with two anchors forward and two aft, and laid up in the charge of a watchman.

19th September 1945: *Samforth*
After sailing from South America to Moss (Norway) and Oslo, the vessel was being assisted by *Ahkera* at Kotka (Finland), when the tug suddenly heeled over to starboard and capsized.

8th October 1945: *Samarovsk*
The ship arrived at Hamburg after a rough crossing from London, during which military vehicles in number 4 'tween deck had broken adrift. Because their petrol tanks were full and battery leads connected, fire had totally destroyed one vehicle and damaged three others as well as the ship.

10th October 1945: *Samaritan*
During her five-day call at the Baltic port of Danzig to discharge cargo from Montreal, the vessel touched bottom on a submerged object, struck the scuttled Italian cargo ship *Africana* (seized by the Germans in 1943) and, on departing for Gdynia, collided with the quayside.

Samaritan after being purchased by Cunard and renamed *Vandalia* (above). Both she and the *City of Leeds* (opposite top) were photgraphed in the Thames by Mr. W. H. Brown. *[W.H. Brown/J. and M. Clarkson collection]*

29th October 1945: *Samtampa*
The day after the ship's departure from the Cape Verde Islands, a stowaway was discovered in the galley coal bunker. When *Samtampa* reached Santos (Brazil) on 8th November, he was jailed for the length of the ship's 13-day stay, then taken into custody again in Rio de Janeiro, when the vessel was diverted there with three port boiler tubes leaking. He was finally handed over to the Cape Verde Island authorities when the ship called homewards on 8th December.

21st November 1945: *Samfaithful*
A donkeyman was investigated at Singapore for entertaining a Japanese officer in his cabin and for supplying cigars to Japanese prisoners-of-war working coal in the holds, but no charges were brought.

22nd November 1945: *Sambre*
Returning to his ship by sampan at Shanghai, an assistant cook was hit by stray bullets fired from the US Landing Ship Dock *Carter Hall*. He died next day aboard the US Hospital Ship *Repose*.

3rd December 1945: *Samhain*
The vessel left Hong Kong having embarked 400 Indian policemen and their dependants bound for Madras.

30th December 1945: *Samflora*
Arriving at Tamatave (Madagascar) in ballast from Mombasa (Kenya), the ship had been instructed to take on board, for passage to Saigon (French Indo-China), military personnel, stores and vehicles of a French Brigade. Accommodation was made available in 16 cabins and for 290 on the troop deck.

17th February 1946: *Sambre*
On passage from Coos Bay (Oregon) to Cardiff, the ship was in danger of being swept by a strong current against a pontoon bridge on departure from Curacao. In weighing anchor in haste, she tore up an underwater cable, thereby severing the area's telephone and radio links.

27th March 1946: *Sambay*
On arrival at Liverpool from the West African ports of Lagos and Takoradi, 18 crew members presented a petition of complaint about the quality and quantity of the food during the seven-month voyage just completed.

1st May 1946: *Samgaudie*
Carrying cargo for Rangoon from Middlesbrough and Hull, the vessel had just left the Humber when her bows became badly damaged in a collision with the US-flag *Andrew Furuseth*. *Samgaudie* put back to Hull the following day with her sailing delayed until 29th June.

9th May 1946: *Samothrace*
While the ship was at Tuticorin (India), 24 crew members mustered on the boat deck to protest at the intolerable heat in the engine room and accommodation. They stated that, if the vessel was to make further voyages to Indian ports without being tropicalised, they would refuse to sail.

10th May 1946: *Samhope*

Sailing through the Magellan Strait in a heavy rain squall on passage from Lourenco Marques (Mozambique) to Tocopilla (Chile), the vessel grounded on a rocky ledge. Although she refloated without assistance on the rising tide after nearly seven hours, bottom damage required temporary repairs at Punta Arenas (Chile), as a prelude to permanent work at Bahia Blanca (Argentina).

10th June 1946: *Ammla*

After a rough passage from Townsville (Australia), the vessel arrived at Hong Kong to land 39 head of cattle. The 40th had died aboard ship, with the carcass being dumped overboard.

28th September 1946: *Samcrest*

Bound from Manchester to Key West (Florida), piston trouble in both feed pumps caused the ship to become totally disabled 24 miles north west of Strumble Head (South Wales). The naval tug *Empire Netta* was summoned to tow her into Milford Haven the following day.

13th October 1946: *Samark*

An accumulation of gases in the furnace, when the starboard boiler was relit at Brindisi (Italy), caused an explosion in the engine room and damage to the boiler casing and furnace. While the ship was still at Brindisi, her Chief Engineer attended an official reception on 20th October but fell to his death from a balcony. During the homeward voyage to Cardiff, a sea search on 30th November failed to find any trace of the Chief Steward, who was missing from the ship and was presumed to have taken his own life by jumping overboard.

21st-26th February 1947: *Samaritan*

While sailing from San Pedro de Macoris (Dominica) to Liverpool with a cargo of raw sugar, prolonged heavy weather resulted in the fracturing of deck and shell plating on the ship's port side.

9th May 1947: *Samhope*

On passage from Tunas de Zaza (Cuba) to the UK at a speed in excess of 10 knots, the ship went firmly aground on a rocky ledge 10 miles from Cape Breton Island (Nova Scotia). Transferring 6,200 bags of sugar into lighters enabled her to refloat after five days.

City of Leeds, formerly the *Samcrest*. *[W.H. Brown/J. and M. Clarkson collection]*

Completion of charter

One of the last of the operational Liberty ships to be returned to the USA was *Samadang* and clearly the requirement in the original agreement, that the vessels remain under the British flag until no later than six months after the termination of the war, was not applied, as none of the vessels was returned in 1945 and only two before 1947. *Samadang*'s service career on charter had lasted four years and three months without major incident. During this time, in addition to berthing at ten different UK terminals, she had crossed the Pacific once and the Atlantic a dozen times. She had transited the Suez Canal on four occasions and the Panama Canal three times and had called at 45 different ports in Australasia; East, South and West Africa; the Far East; India; the Mediterranean; South America; the West Indies and the Atlantic and Pacific coasts of North America. To conclude her Red Ensign service, the ship left London on 18th June 1948 and reached New Orleans on 22nd July, in preparation for return to the US Maritime Commission nine days later. She was then moved for lay-up at Beaumont (Texas) on 9th August and, without seeing further service, was scrapped 20 years later.

Of the original 182 Liberty ships taken over by Britain, around two-thirds were sold for further service, mostly with the British companies responsible for their wartime management. These articles have been intended to give an insight into the part these invaluable ships played, not only in the later stages of the Second World War, but also in the difficult early post-war years, highlighting a selection of the cargoes they carried, some of the ports they served, many of the hazards they encountered and a number of the incidents in which they were involved.

After being totally disabled during a September 1946 voyage from Manchester to the USA, *Samcrest*, seen above at New Plymouth, New Zealand was towed into Milford Haven by a naval tug. *[Ian J. Farquhar]*

PRINCE LINE FOLLOW-UP

Warrior Prince

I note that in 'Record' 41 you are looking for suggestions about the naval service of *Stuart Prince*. I hope that the following may be of use.

On completion she was taken over by Government and was operated by the Liner Division. I understand that this meant that her owners ran her under Government orders as to cargoes loaded and voyages.

According to the 'Convoy Web' she arrived in Liverpool on 9th May 1943. This is the last entry in the Convoy Web. This would fit with your stating that she was then required for 'Miscellaneous Naval Service'.

I think that she was then converted to a Landing Ships Fighter Direction (LSF). Lenton on page 448 of 'British and Empire Warships of the Second World War' states that the converted merchant ships were 'fitted out as landing ships fighter direction/LSFs with AW RDF, air plots, R/T communications, so that enemy air counter attacks against invading forces could be detected, plotted, and the defending fighter aircraft vectored into an intercept position'.

I think that she took a long time to fit-out and the next information I have is that she took part in Operation Dragoon (National Archives file AIR 23/7258). This is also mentioned on pages 36 and 117 of 'British Invasion Fleets' by John de S. Winser which states that she left Ajaccio on 14th August and served as a beacon for the airborne assault and as air-sea rescue ship, and as a fighter direction and radar ship.

She is then mentioned as being in Convoy MKS 65 from the Mediterranean to UK, sailing on 27th October 1944 and arriving on 7th November 1944 (National Archives file ADM 199/2193/6). She is not mentioned in the Convoy Web under MKS 65. I think that the photograph was taken about this time or early 1945. Given the Royal Navy's manning problem at this time I suspect that she was 'Returned to Trade' or, possibly, used as a training ship.

The DEMS hut mentioned beneath the post-war photograph must have been fitted after she returned from the Mediterranean and before VE-day as it would not have been fitted post-VE day. Therefore she was returned to trade in late 1944 or early 1945.

DAVID TRANTER, Cedars, 1 Upgate, Poringland, Norfolk NR14 7SH

George Swaine, author of the Prince Line articles, notes that between 1940 and 1943 Stuart Prince *made three voyages to the West Indies followed by 13 consecutive transatlantic voyages, all without incident, and was then requisitioned at Liverpool. Ed.*

Scruffy Prince

Thank you for the very interesting 'Record' 43. I would comment that, contrary to Prince Line's apparently usual high standards, *Eastern Prince* as *Bardic* when visited at Avonmouth in the early 1960s was in poor condition with a filthy engine room - in stark contrast to the Liberty *Maria Stathatos* visited around the same time (albeit she had only recently resumed trading after a period of lay up which had presumably allowed time for maintenance).

MALCOLM CRANFIELD, 8 Foxcover Road, Heswall, Wirral L60 ITB

Watchful Prince

Page 136, middle photo of *Chinese Prince*. The cylindrical construction on the bridge (between the DF loop and the signal mast) is, in fact, a radar aerial of the Admiralty type. These were fitted to some merchant ships during the war - the scanner itself was totally enclosed in fibreglass or plastic. This is more clearly visible in the lower picture of the same ship on page 135. The replacement, a more conventional Decca radar scanner, is also just visible in the later photo of the ship as *Nordic*.

Page 137, *Javanese Prince*. The tug pictured did not look like a South African tug and I then noticed that the courtesy flag flying from the signal mast amidships (and only partly obscured by Flag H signifying 'pilot on board') was the Stars and Stripes.

DAVID WITTRIDGE, 25 Fairlawn Close, Rownhams, Southampton SO16 8DT

In the middle photograph on page 136, the *Chinese Prince* still has her Type 272 or 273 radar lantern atop the bridge.

BOB TODD, National Maritime Museum, Greenwich, London SE10 9NF

George Swaine notes that a Decca 159 radar was fitted at Taikoo Dockyard, Hong Kong whilst the ship was on the round-the-world service, probably around 1948. The Admiralty installation had been partially dismantled. Ed

Not the Italian Princes

I found the interesting and well illustrated article on Prince Line an addition to our knowledge. I like detail of the actual trading an important adjunct to a company history, which is unfortunately often lacking. The following is *not* a criticism.

There is a strong belief among some maritime historians (and repeated in 'Record' 41) that Prince Line ordered two twin-screw passenger ships from the Sunderland shipbuilder Sir James Laing and Sons and that during construction this contract was taken over by Lloyd Sabaudo of Genoa. In fact these ships (yard numbers 621, 622 and 623) were ordered and built for the Italian company and all were completed in 1907.

The only reference to James Knott and Prince Line in connection with these ships is in a Prince Line fleet list in the Newcastle newspapers for September 1908, which lists the *Sardinian Prince* and *Piedmontese Prince* as being at Naples (and for one week only).

There is a strong possibility (however, no actual evidence) that Prince Line considered chartering two of the Lloyd Sabaudo vessels due to increased competition and rising costs in the Mediterranean emigrant trade, combined with the Italian government subsidising its own merchant fleet. The other piece of evidence is the well-known Prince Line advertisement clearly showing a steamer with two funnels.

JOHN DOBSON, 48 Cochrane Park Avenue, Newcastle-upon-Tyne NE7 7JU

The author comments: Mr Dobson makes an interesting point. In contemporary company documents (1907), James Knott refers to this order. There is no evidence as to when title transferred although received wisdom is that construction actually commenced under the aegis of Prince Line but was transferred at an early stage to Sabaudo. Whether this was merely a commercial 'guarantee of payment to the shipbuilder' arrangement is not known and, due to lack of records, probably never will be.

The *Cyprian Prince* (1) built by Shorts, Sunderland in 1878 and acquired by Prince Line in 1899 is shown in February 1905 as the first vessel to berth alongside the newly constructed deep water wharf at Famagusta. At that time, although the island was still nominally within the Ottoman Empire, it had been occupied by Britain since 1878 under treaty arrangements to guard the northern approaches to the Suez Canal. These harbour works, which ran parallel to the southern fortifications of the Venetian city, were the first to be undertaken for at least 400 years.

The *Cyprian Prince* (1) did not have a lengthy career under James Knott's ownership. Three years after the above photograph she was wrecked during thick fog on the Farilhoes Islands, northwest of Lisbon. *[K. Vassiliou/George Swaine collection via Alec Henderson]*

Taken from virtually the same position as the above photograph but 51 years later in November 1956, this shows three Prince Line ships, *Cyprian Prince* (4), *Black Prince* (4) and *Maltese Prince* (1), plus an unidentified Ellerman Papayanni vessel. Despite cosmetic differences, cargo handling methods remained practically unchanged in the half century between the two photographs, although they were soon to change out of all recognition. *[Prince Line /George Swaine collection via Alec Henderson]*

BOSUN'S LOCKER

What a great response to the unidentified photographs in "Record' 43. I think it was the first time we had shown so many but even so, the response was fantastic. Keep it up. We will come back to them shortly and we have a few new ones for you to consider. We would have had more to show you but again space has beaten us.

When researching photographs to illustrate articles in 'Record' we have a number of regular contacts. If all else fails we turn to the museum collections but only as a last resort. It is now almost impossible, due to low staffing levels, for them to check on a particular ship and they suggest that such requests be in writing - replies often taking a considerable time. The Maritime Museum at Barrow is great, one can go on line, search and bring up thumbnail images. Orders are then supplied within a few days on a CD or as prints. The Imperial War Museum have a similar arrangement which works well although it is admitted that it only covers about 10,000 images, a small percentage of their total holding. The National Maritime Museum appear to have got a new website - have any of you tried it out? If not, perhaps some of you would like to, and at the same time for comparison, having a look at the IWM site. We would be interested to have feedback from you as to how you find them and what problems you encountered along the way.

Now back to pictures for identification. In 'Record' 43 we posted eight photographic problems, and for all but one we have solutions provided by our extremely knowledgeable readership, to whom we are most grateful.

43/01. The device 'shaped like a fob watch' on the funnel of this early bulk carrier turns out to have been a stylised letter G, and the markings are those of United States Gypsum Company of New York. Bill Schell tells us the ship was one of a quartet completed between 1927 and 1929 by Furness Shipbuilding Co., purpose built for carrying gypsum rock from the mines in Nova Scotia to plaster-board plants on the U.S. East Coast. *Gypsum King*, *Gypsum Prince* and *Gypsum Queen* were completed in 1927 and there was a follow-on order for *Gypsum Empress*, delivered in 1929. They were all Middlesbrough registered, but the crews were very heavily Canadian. Registered owner was the Gypsum Packet Co. Ltd. of Windsor, Nova Scotia, which was a subsidiary of the United States Gypsum Company of New York. Only *Gypsum King* survived the Second World War, serving her original owners until sold in 1961.

The U. S. Gypsum plant in Boston was in Charlestown just inside the mouth of the Mystic River and only recently became idle. The ships discharged there by shore grabs. The more recent vessels in the fleet were self-unloaders, discharging by a short belt which poked out of a sideport in the stern and met a low hopper on the wharf.

Thanks also to Christy MacHale and Bob Todd for identifying this funnel marking. Christy made the eminently sensible point that the difference between the four ships was in the length of their second names: four, five, six and seven letters, respectively. On this basis, and looking at the original print the likelihood is that the ship depicted is *Gypsum King*.

43/02. Readers who identified this steamer as the whaleback *City of Everett* included Colin Turner, Dick Pryde, Bill Schell, Bob Todd and John Wilterding. There is quite a story to her.

The only whaleback built on the Pacific coast, *City of Everett* was completed in 1894 at the town after which she was named in Washington state. Builder was the American Steel Barge Company (yard number 145) for their own account and who registered her at Port Townsend, Washington. Construction seems to have been a protracted affair. A local newspaper reported that in December 1891 a Captain Alexander McDougal, described as the 'inventor of the barge', arrived in Everett. Also that month another whaleback, the *Charles W. Wetmore*, arrived at the town carrying material for the construction of *City of Everett* which had been loaded in East Coast ports and brought round Cape Horn.

She passed in December 1901 to Standard Oil Company of New York who had *City of Everett* converted to a tanker, and photograph 43/02 showed her in Standard Oil's funnel colours, with her hatch covers open to ventilate the cargo spaces. The photograph was evidently taken between 1901 and 1903 as on 8th September 1903 at the Texas Company's berth at Port Arthur, Texas she exploded. When rebuilt in 1904 at Brooklyn, New York she was lengthened and fitted with an orthodox bow and stern.

Standard Oil sold her in November 1922 and she went into the molasses trade, owned by Abram I. Kaplan of New York. She lasted less than a year. Still named *City of Everett* she sailed from Santiago de Cuba for New Orleans on 7th October 1923 with a crew of 26 and four days later foundered during a hurricane in the Gulf of Mexico.

43/03. The location of the sunken paddle steamer is definitely the inside of the east arm of the Victoria Pier at Hull. There is still some uncertainty over the vessel involved, but readers have narrowed it down to two. Alan Savory has in his collection an identical card on which a previous owner has written 'The old *Doncaster* as seen in the Humber at half tide'. *Doncaster* was built at Hull in 1855 and worked as a Humber ferry for a remarkable 58 years, being withdrawn about 1913 (possibly after the incident shown). Bob Todd offers the suggestion that she may be the *Manchester*, built in 1876 by the Goole Shipbuilding and Engineering Company, which operated as a Humber goods ferry until 1914. The only photograph Bob can find to back up this supposition is a starboard bow view in which everything seems to fit but he cannot see the stern cabin which prominent in the photograph. The vessel is undoubtedly a Humber ferry, and the balance of probability is *Doncaster*, but we await confirmation.

43/04. This photograph has resulted in us being given more information than all the other queries in 'Record' 43 put together, and it turns out that our guesses that it could be a tender or pilot boat and was off Douglas, Isle of Man were both quite wrong. The photograph was taken in the Channel Islands and shows a well-known local vessel. Robert Langlois and Dave Hocquard have come up with extensive information on both location and the vessel, which became a household name in the islands.

It shows the 151gt *Courier* which was completed in May 1883 at Southampton by Day, Summers and Co. Ltd. as yard number 68 for the Alderney Steam Packet Co. Ltd. (Thomas N. Barbenson, manager), Guernsey. She was built to run between St. Peter Port, Guernsey and Braye Harbour, Alderney as a passenger and supply ship for the northernmost Channel Island, and also provided day excursions to the other Channel Islands. *Courier* had various owners over the years, in 1919 for instance owners became the Guernsey, Alderney and Sark Steamship Co. Ltd. (J.G. Piprell and Sons, managers) of St. Peter Port.

Courier struck a rock in the Percee Passage between Herm and Jethouon 1905 and was beached on the small islet of Crevichon, but was soon refloated and returned to service. A more serious incident occurred on 30th April 1906 when *Courier* struck the Les Amons Rocks south of Jethou and sank with the loss of 10 lives from the 39 passengers and crew aboard. In July 1906 she was refloated and taken to St. Peter Port where she was made fit to be towed to Southampton to be repaired by her builders.

In June 1940 *Courier* was the last ship to leave Guernsey before the Germans arrived. She was laid up in the River Dart for some time before being sent to the Clyde for service as a tender to Royal Navy ships, as which she was renamed HMS *Caracole*. In 1945 she returned to lay up in the River Dart and remained there until the spring of 1947 when sold to a new company, Sark Projects Ltd., of Guernsey. After an overhaul at Cosens' yard at Weymouth she returned to Guernsey renamed *Courier*, arriving on 11th July 1947 to a tumultuous welcome. She restarted her old route to Sark and Alderney but ran for only about a month. Age and hard work had caught up with her and she was laid up in St. Sampson Harbour until November 1947 when she left Guernsey for the last time bound for Shoreham and further lay up. She was sold to Dutch breakers in 1948 and demolished later that year. David recalls that he was very lucky to have travelled to Sark on a day excursion on the *Courier* in late July 1947 while on holiday with parents in Guernsey.

Robert has also gone to considerable trouble to identify the viewpoint for photograph 43/04, which shows *Courier* arriving at St. Peter Port. It was taken looking north north west from near the end of the southern breakwater which protects the harbour and which projects out into the Little Russel. In the background is a reef known as Goubeau carrying a conical beacon, whilst to the right is a smaller rock known as Sardrette surmounted with a pole. The tall chimney in the distance is that of Guernsey's original power station, which was demolished early in the twentieth century, confirming that 43/04 was taken well before the First World War, and probably shows *Courier* in original condition.

Reproduced here (above) is a further photograph of *Courier* which Robert kindly supplied and is believed to show her in the 1930s, after considerable modification. She

has a wheel house, her accommodation has been extended aft and extra lifeboats added. The legend 'Royal Mail' was carried on her superstructure, surmounted by a crown. This photograph may have been taken by Thomas Westness of Alderney.

Thanks also to John Pryce and Stephen Carter for their thoughts on image 43/04.

43/05. The paddler is Cosen's veteran *Premier* (129/1846) entering Weymouth harbour, probably around 1900. She was built by William Denny and Brothers at Dumbarton for the Dumbarton Steamboat Company who ran her between Glasgow and Dumbarton. She must have been one of the first iron ships built by Denny as the yard had built their first only in the previous year. In 1852 she was sold to a Mr. Tizard of Weymouth who ran her from Weymouth in direct competition with Cosens until the two operations merged about 1860. In 1878 *Premier* returned to the Clyde for lengthening by just three feet. Her original steeple engine was replaced by an oscillating engine and her funnels reduced to one. Remarkably, she remained in service until 1939 when she was sold to T.W. Ward Ltd. for just £290. The Hull tug *Brahman* towed her out of Weymouth on 29th April bound for Ward's yard at Grays, Essex. Thanks to Dave Hocquard, Geoff Holmes and K.C. Saunders for this information.

43/06. Tony Smythe reckons this *Curlew* was built by J.S. White at Cowes in 1904, yard number 1182. A single screw launch of 64 feet, she was one of five built between 1903 and 1904 for The Crown Agent, Nigeria. The others were *Magpie* (yard number 1166), *Hawk* (1167), *Owl* (1168) and *Snipe* (1183).

43/07. It is unlikely we will be able to put a name to the topsail schooner unless someone comes up with another copy of this photograph on which it is identified. However, Captain Stephen Carter has identified the tug *Iris*. It belonged to J.H. Lamey and was built as a steam yacht at Glasgow in 1892 for James Coates of sewing cotton fame. At this time the small Lamey fleet had a plain black funnel with a white letter L. It was not until later that the company adopted the more familiar black, white and red funnel with the black letter L, still seen today on Laxey Towing Company vessels. *Iris* is probably towing a china clay-laden schooner up the Mersey to Runcorn or Weston Point.

43/08. Captain John Anderson tells us that there is a photo which appears to show the same incident on page 218 of 'Sea Breezes' for March 1926. It occurred in 1923 at Calcutta, and John notes that the ships are moored with chain suggesting strong currents. The four-masted barque is the German *Lemkenhaven* (2,277/1892) built by Russell and Company, Greenock as *Donna Francisca*, and uncommonly fitted with water ballast tanks. Sold to J.G.H. Seimers of Hamburg in 1910, she was renamed *Herbert* and became *Lemkenhaven* in 1922 when she passed to Schröder, Hölken and Fischer, also of Hamburg. She was wrecked on 4th June 1924 near Cerro Azul, Peru for which port she was bound with coal from Newcastle, New South Wales. Lubbock credits the ship with some good passages, partly attributed to short port stays and a clean hull due the water ballast facility. The steamer on which *Lemkenhaven* is leaning is *Grelarlie* (3,580/1910). The former *Rachel*, she carried this name from 1918 to 1924. Thanks also to John Naylon for thoughts on this image.

44/01. This photograph is of a steam coaster owned by the appropriately named Thomas Miller Collier, seen entering Bray, County Wicklow where Collier was based. Photographs of ships in his distinctive funnel colours are rare, but with a fleet of 11 ships, all of which had previous or subsequent owners, it is possible to eliminate many candidates by comparison with other photographs. There are two possibilities.

Braedale (1) ex-*Breaksea* was built at Goole in 1911 and was owned by Collier from 1911 to 1915. She was 143 feet long.

Braefield was formerly *Ithfaen* and *Maggie Bain*, and was later renamed *Ashford*. Built by Scotts of Bowling in 1892 and 160 feet long, she was owned only briefly, between 1915 and being sunk in 1917, and would probably have been painted grey.

Assuming the eliminations are correct, and based on length, the most likely candidate is *Braedale* (1), but confirmation is requested.

44/02. This negative I put aside many years ago thinking it was of a building with a maritime use and of no interest at the time. When I came across it recently I thought that maybe one of our readers would know where it is, or was. After scanning the negative I was surprised to see that it is of a ship, upside down and being broken up. So now the question is - which ship and where is she? No doubt she is one of the German High Seas Fleet, sunk at Scapa Flow and later raised. I wonder how they got those timber supports under the forward end?

44/03. Our last picture is well documented. It was sent to a newspaper with details of the occasion attached. The caption tells us that the huge floating dock, being towed into Portsmouth, will make a valuable addition to the dry-docking of warships at Portsmouth. The dock arrived in Spithead on 21st August 1912 after a rough voyage of a week from Birkenhead where it had been built by Cammell Laird. Due to bad weather the dock was only brought into Portsmouth harbour on 22nd. The dock was 700 feet long with a length of 680 feet over the blocks. It could lift 40,000 tons - 800 tons more than a similar dock delivered to the Medway and will take the most recent super-dreadnoughts yet built or designed.

The question is - does anyone know the identity of the pictured lead tug - one of Jolliffe's perhaps?

INDEX TO RECORD 41 TO 44
Issue numbers are shown in bold

Index of articles

Index of ships

All ships' names are listed, including proposed or other names not actually used, which are shown in brackets.

270

Malika 44:262
Malplaquet 42:88-9
Maltese Prince (1946)
  41:4-5,13; 42:67; 44:265
Malvern Prince (1970)
  42:70-1,75
Mana 43:158
Manara 42:76
Manchester (1876) 44:266
Manchester Crown 42:79
Manchester Trader 43:144-5
Mandagala 43:139
Mandraki 42:72
Manioglu 44:243
Mano 41:20
Manoora (1936) 43:161
Mansoor (1940) 43:193
Maplebank 42:113
Marabank 42:111
Marc I 43:155
Margalau (1926) 41:52
Margaret Clunies
  43:173-4,176,179-80,182
(Margaret Waterston) 41:18
Margrid II 43:155
Mari 42:72
Maria B 42:70
Maria de Larrinaga 42:107
Maria Stathatos 44:264
Maria 41:6
Marianne Clunies (1918)
  43:175-80,183
Mariber 42:72
Marietta Dal 42:108-9
Marilaki 41:26
Marine Carrier 43:139
Mariner 43:144
Marinex III 42:92
Marion (tug) 44:228
Markella II 43:153
Marta 43:157
Mary Moller 42:107
Maryston 41:44;44:233
Mathios Apessakis 41:26
Matrona 44:225
Maulabaksh 41:51
Maxton 41:62
Medic 43:144
Medway (1902) 42:117,122
Meera 43:152
Meeraa 43:152
Megaluck 42:101
Melina 43:152
Mendip (HMS) 44:259
Mendip Prince (1970)
  42:70,76,79
Menelaus (1957) 44:248,252
Mentor (5) (1977) 44:253
Merauke (1912) 41:61
Mercator 41:62
Merchant Prince (3) (1950)
  41:5-6,14
Merryland 44:206
Merve 44:244
Meteor (1888) 42:124
Middleton (HMS) 43:167
Mikelden 42:96
Mill Hill 42:109
Milos 41:15
Mimi 41:7
Mimi-M 41:6
Mirabelle (HMS) 44:258
Mistley (1) (1922)
  41:44;44:222-3
Mistley (2) (1920)
  41:47;44:223-5,272
Miteria Eirini 44:243
Moderator 42:106
Monarch of Bermuda
  43:137,139
Monowai 43:197
Montañes (1878) 42:127
Mountpark 44:242
Mozambique 44:211
MP-ZP-GDY-6 42:105
Mr Louie 41:56
Mull 43:150
Mullion Cove 43:173,182
Mustansir (1949) 43:193
Myra Fell 41:63
Myrina 41:31-2
Myrshell (1902) 42:117,122
Myrsini 42:90
M-ZP-GDY-6 42:105

Nader 3 42:76
Nadia 1 43:157
Naftilos 42:72;44:210
Nanina 41:24
Nasser 43:159
Navajo (tug) 41:19
Ndoni River 42:101
Nestor (4) (1952) 44:251
Nestor (5) (1977) 44:253
Nestor II 41:15
Nevsehir 44:236-7
Newcastle Star 41:52
Newfoundland (1948)
  41:5;43:137,139
Nialed Trader 43:155
Nic 42:95
Nicholas (1974) 42:101
Nikola Tesla 42:109
Nikolas K 41:16
Nikos 43:158
Nnamdi Azikiwe (1963)
  41:22,27;42:93-5; 44:221
Nomad 41:45
Norah Moller 42:109
Nordic 43:136;44:264
Norman Prince (5) (1956)
  42:67-8,74
Norman Prince (4) (1940)
  41:4
North Cornwall 41:1,20-1,24
Northern Archer 44:244
Northern Firth 41:48
Northford 41:46
Northleigh 44:260
Northumbrian Prince (2)
(1956) 42:66-7,74
Nova Scotia (1947)
  41:5;43:137,139
Oba Overami (1948)
  41:22,29
Oba Ovonramwen
  41:22-3,29;42:93
Ocean Monarch 43:137,139
Oceanic Wave 43:139
Oceanus (tug) 42:127
Odemis 44:240
Oduduwa (1954)
  41:1,20,22,24;42:93-4
Ogun 42:99
Omar 42:74
Onehunga 42:77
Onto Star 42:79
OOCL Ambition 42:79
Ophir 44:262
Orangemoor (1911) 43:171
Oranmore (1895)
  41:45-7;44:233
Oranyan (1953)
  41:22,26;42:93-4
Oregon Star 42:107
Orient Ganges 42:100
Orient Prosperity 43:144
Orient Trader 43:139
Ornella 41:10
Ortinashell (1891)
  42:117-8,122-3
Osunic 1 (1969) 43:152
Oweenee (1891)
  42:117,122-3
Owl (tug) 43:164
Owl (1904) 44:267
Oxfordshire (2) (1957)
  44:209
P. Dolores 42:74
P.L. Pahlsson 43:168
Pachitea 41:54-5
Pacific Endeavour 43:189
Pacific Importer 42:112
Pacific Liberty 42:107
Pacific Nomad 42:107
Pacific Ranger 42:107
Pacific Star 42:111
Pacific Stronghold 43:139
Pacific Unity 41:53
Pakistan Prosperity (1926)
  41:52
Palestinian Prince (1) (1936)
  41:2-3,5,7;42:67
Pamela C 42:91
Pamela 42:77
Pannesi 44:231
Parana Star 42:77
Parkesgate 43:157
Parma (1967) 44:228

Parnon 43:192
Parrot 42:94
Pass of Balmaha 41:19
Patric M 43:152
Patricia 43:190
Pearl 43:150
Pearlmead (1905) 43:171
Pearlmoor (1897) 43:171
Pearlmoor (1905) 43:171
Peisander (1967) 44:250
Peleus (1949) 44:248-9
Pembrokeshire (1967)
  44:250
Penang (sailing vessel)
  44:234
Pennine Prince (1971)
  42:71,78
Pentire 42:110
Perseus (1950) 44:248;254
Petro Minor 42:92
Petro Soulac 42:101
Phaedra 42:78
Phassa 42:109
Phorkyss 43:180
Piedmontese Prince (1907)
  42:71;44:264
Pinemore (1955) 42:67,73
Pinmore 41:19
Plancius 42:91
Poeldyk 42:94,96
Poldhu 42:82,87
Poole Harbour 42:89,44:235
Port Albany 42:111
Port Chalmers 43:170
Port Hardy 44:206
Port Invercargill
  41:60;44:227
Port Jackson 42:117
Portmarnock (1962) 43:157
Posidon (tug) 41:62
Premier (1846) 44:267
President Magsaysay 43:182
Priam (4) (1943) 44:246
Primrose Hill 42:109
Princess Immela 43:157
Prizeman (tug) 43:166
Prophecy 41:31
Protesilaus (1967) 44:250
Pulborough 42:125
Pythomene 41:17
Quan 42:79
Queen of Bermuda
  43:137,139
Queen Victoria 42:107
Queens Channel (1894)
  42:81
Rachel (1910) 44:268
Radnorshire (1967) 44:250
Rakaia 41:61
Rania G (tug) 42:126
Rashidah 42:76
Rathlin 43:166
Ravensworth (1883)
  41:63;42:127
Re d'Italia 42:71
Regina d'Italia 42:71
Renown (tug) 42:128
Repose (US hospital ship)
  44:262
Resilient 42:98
Resolve (1946) (tug) 42:126
Reynolds 42:107
Rhexenor (1945) 44:246
Richard Hovey 44:255
Richmond Castle (1944)
  42:125
Riebeeck Castle 42:124
Risaldar 41:51
River (1968) 42:93
River (1979) 42:100
River Aboine 42:96,101
River Adada
  42:95,97-8,100,102
River Andoni 42:97-8
River Asab 42:97-8
River Benue 42:93-5
River Ethiope
  42:93-5;44:219-20
River Gongola 42:94-6
River Guma 42:95-6
River Gurara 42:95-6,102
River Hadejia 42:94-5,100
River Ikpan 42:97-8,102
River Jimini 42:95-7,100

River Mada 42:97-8
River Maje 42:96-8
River Majidun
  42:95,97-8,101
River Ngada 42:95,97-8
River Niger 42:93-5
River Ogbese 42:96-8
River Ogun 42:93-5,99
River Oji 42:97-8,101
River Oli 42:97-8
River Oshun 42:97-8
River Osse 42:97-8
River Rima 42:96
Riverina (1905) 42:128
Rockferry 43:194
Rockpool 41:53
Rodania 42:74
Rogate 42:125
Rondeau Park 44:254
Ronhill 41:27
Ronson 41:27
Roodebeek 43:159
Rora Head (1921) 43:153
Rosalie Moller 42:109
Rosana R 41:53
Rose (tug) 44:256
Rose I 43:157
Roseburn (1947) 42:89-90
Rosehill (1966) 43:152
Roseland (1961) 43:150
Roselyne (1) (1939)
  42:82,87;44:224
Roselyne (2) (1955) 42:91;
  43:159;44:223,235
Rosemarkie (1) (1939)
  42:82,88-9;44:234
Rosemarkie (2) (1957)
  42:92
Rosemount (1967)
  43:150-1
Roseneath (1949)
  42:89,44:235
Rosewell (1950)
  42:90,44:235
Rowanbank 42:111
Rowanmore (2) 43:143
Rowland T. Delano 44:244
Roxburgh Castle (1937)
  42:125
Royal Prince (5) (1979)
  42:71,79
Ruby (1854) 42:127
Rudby 42:112
Rupsa 43:193
Rustenburg Castle 42:124
S. Manioglu 44:237
Safina-e-Haider 44:213
Sailor Prince (1971)
  42:71,78
Sajany 42:110
Salmonier 42:110
Saltersgate 43:191;44:227
Salvage Chieftain
  43:165,169
Salvager 1 42:90
Salveda 43:165
Samadang 42:106-7;44:263
Samadre 42:107;44:254
Samaffric 42:107
Samakron 42:107
Samalness 42:107
Samana 44:258
Samannan 42:107;43:166
Samara 42:104,107,112
Samarina 42:107;44:259
Samarinda 42:107
Samaritan 42:103-4,107;
  43:166;44:262-3
Samariz 42:104,107
Samark 42:107;44:260,263
Samarkand
  42:107;44:254,261
Samarovsk
  42:107;44:255,262
Samaustral 42:107;44:261
Samavon 42:107;44:258
Samaye 42:107
Sambalt 42:107
Sambanka 42:107;44:254
Sambay 42:107;44:262
Samblade 42:107;43:162-3
Sambo 42:107;43:162-3
Samboston 42:65,107
Sambrake 42:107

Sambre 42:107;44:256,262
Sambrian 42:107;44:254
Sambridge
  42:103,106-7;43:163
Sambuff 42:104-5,107
Sambur 42:104,107
Samburgh 42:107
Sambuss 42:107
Sambut 42:107;43:164
Samcalia
  42:107;43:166;44:255-6
Samcebu 42:107
Samchess 42:107;44:259-60
Samcleve 42:107
Samclyde 42:107
Samconon 42:106-7
Samconstant 42:107;43:166
Samcree 42:107;44:261
Samcrest 42:107;44:263
Samdak 42:103,107
Samdaring 42:104,107
Samdart 42:107
Samdauntless 42:107
Samdee 42:109
Samdel 42:104,109;43:166
Samderry 42:109
Samderwent 42:109;44:261
Samdon 42:109;44:262
Samdonard
  41:54;42:109;44:259
Samearn 42:108-9
Sameden 42:109
Samesk 42:109
Samettrick 42:109
Sameveron 42:109;44:258-9
Samfairy 42:109
Samfaithful 42:109;44:262
Samfeugh 42:109
Samfield 42:109;44:259
Samfinn 42:109
Samfleet 42:109
Samflora 42:109;44:262
Samforth 42:109;44:255,262
Samfoyle 42:109;44:256
Samfreedom 42:109
Samfyne 42:112
Samgallion 42:108-9
Samgara 42:109;43:166;
  44:255,261-2
Samgaudie 42:109;44:262
Samglory 42:109;44:260-1
Samhain 42:109;44:262
Samharle 42:109
Samholt
  42:103,109;44:254,260
Samhope
  42:109;44:258,260,263
Samhorn 42:109;44:258
Samida
  42:109;43:167;44:256
Samidway
  42:109;43:166;44:254
Samindoro 42:109;42:113
Samingoy 42:108-9
Saminver
  42:109;44:254,259-60
Samite 42:109;43:162-4
Samjack
  42:104,109;43:168;44:254
Samkansa 42:109
Samkey
  42:109;43:170;44:258
Samlamu 42:104-5,110
Samlea 42:110;44:258
Samleven 42:110
Samleyte 42:110;44:254
Samlistar 42:110;43:168
Samlong
  42:110;43:165;44:255
Samlorian 42:110
Samlossie 42:110
Samlouis 42:110
Samloyal 42:110;43:166
Samluzon 42:110
Samlyth 42:110;43:166
Sammex 42:110
Sammont
  42:110;44:256,258
Samneagh 42:110;44:261
Samnebra 42:110;44:254,257
Samnegros 42:110
Samnesse 42:110
Samnethy 42:110;43:166
Samneva 42:111;43:164

A last look at *Mistley* (2) in the colours of W.N. Lindsay: see 'A tale of two *Mistleys*' by Douglas J. Lindsay on page 222 of this issue. *[Douglas J. Lindsay collection]*